Y0-EFE-340

# HEBE'S STORY

For
Fernando Coronil,
with warm regards.
Pat Steiner

# HEBE'S STORY

## THE INSPIRING RISE AND DISMAYING EVOLUTION OF THE MOTHERS OF THE PLAZA DE MAYO

### Patricia Owen Steiner

Copyright © 2003 by Patricia Owen Steiner.

Library of Congress Number:          2003093594
ISBN :          Hardcover          1-4134-1242-4
                Softcover          1-4134-1241-6

All rights reserved. No part of this book may be reproduced or transmitted in
any form or by any means, electronic or mechanical, including photocopying,
recording, or by any information storage and retrieval system, without permission
in writing from the copyright owner.

This book was printed in the United States of America.

To order additional copies of this book, contact:
Xlibris Corporation
1-888-795-4274
www.Xlibris.com
Orders@Xlibris.com
19292

**For us the true cemetery is memory.**

—Rodolfo J. Walsh

# SOURCE ABBREVIATIONS

AD    —Diago-*Conversando con las Madres de Plaza de Mayo*
AR    —*The Argentina Reader*
EN    —Endnote
HM    —*Historia de Las Madres de Plaza de Mayo*
HV    —1—Verbitsky—*Rodolfo Walsh y la prensa clandestina (1976-1978)*
HV    —2—Verbitsky—*The Flight*
HV    —3—Verbitsky—article in *Pagina 12*
JLA    —Anderson—*Che Guevara*
LL    —*Las Locas* magazine
MB    —Bouvard—*Revolutionary Motherhood*
MPM    —*Mothers of the Plaza de Mayo* newspaper
MF    —Feitlowitz—*A Lexicon of Terror*
NM    —*Nunca Más*
NYT    —*The New York Times*
OAS    —Organization of American States, International Commission on Human Rights, *Report on the Situation of Human Rights in Argentina*
RJW    —Walsh—*El violento oficio de escribir*

# OTHER ABBREVIATIONS USED IN TEXT

**AI**        —Amnesty International

**ANCLA**—Agency for Clandestine News

**AVT**      —Association of Victims of Terrorism. A Spanish group
        opposed to ETA

**CONADEP**—Argentine National Commission on the Disappeared

**ESMA** —Naval Mechanics School

**ETA**      —A terrorist group fighting for independence of the
        Basque region of Spain

**OAS**      —Organization of American States

# Contents

Preface ............................................................................... 10

Introduction ...................................................................... 12

## PART ONE

## HEBE'S STORY AND THE EARLY DAYS OF THE MOTHERS OF THE PLAZA DE MAYO

### CHILDHOOD AND MARRIAGE

Chapter 1: Snapshots of A Childhood .................................... 18

Chapter 2: Marriage and Motherhood .................................... 29

Chapter 3: Hitting Home ........................................................ 44

### REACTIONS AND REALITY

Chapter 4: Hebe and the Plaza de Mayo ................................ 66

Chapter 5: The Mothers' Early Actions ................................... 76

Chapter 6: Discovering the Truth ........................................... 84

Chapter 7: Horrendous Days ................................................. 90

# A NEW PHASE

Chapter 8: Gaining Visibility .............................................. 104

Chapter 9: Word From Prisons ........................................... 120

Chapter 10: The Mothers Gain Confidence
    and a New Mission .......................................... 130

Chapter 11: The End of an Era ........................................... 143

Coda I: The Mothers As Seen in 1983 ............................... 149

## PART TWO

## THE EVOLUTION OF THE MOTHERS OF THE PLAZA DE MAYO AFTER 1983

## THE MOTHERS UNDER DEMOCRATIC GOVERNMENTS

Chapter 12: The Government of
    Raúl Alfonsín (1983-1989) ........................................... 154

Chapter 13: The Government of
    Carlos Menem (1989-1999) ......................................... 170

Chapter 14: The Government of Fernando
    De La Rúa (1999-2001) ................................................ 183

Coda II: The Mothers As Seen in 2003 .............................. 199


Endnotes .......................................................................... 204

Selected Bibliography ........................................................ 216

# PREFACE

$B$ooks are seldom really written by just one person. The idea for the book may have started in the mind of a single individual, but for the transformation of that idea into a coherent book, the "author" relies on the influence of many people. For me there have been several writers over the past three years who have offered the pivotal information and insights that have helped to form and later transform my original perception both of Hebe de Bonafini and of the Mothers of the Plaza de Mayo and have enabled me to bring this book to a convinced conclusion.

The initial influence came from Gabriela Nouzeilles who invited me to translate a brief excerpt from Hebe's autobiography for *The Argentina Reader* (Duke University Press, 2002). This led me to read the whole of the Spanish autobiography.

I am greatly indebted to Matilde Sanchez who edited and played a large role in the writing of Hebe's early story (*Historias de Vida*, Buenos Aires, 1985). She was my gracious liaison with Hebe and facilitated my getting permission to translate and publish Hebe's story.

In my growing realization of the far different side of the Mothers that emerges in Part II, I later studied Marguerite Guzman Bouvard's *Revolutionary Motherhood* (Scholarly Resources, 1994). I am grateful to her both for pin-pointing the co-option of the Mothers' movement by young radicals of the Front for Human Rights and for first alerting me to the Mothers' formal espousal of anarchism.

It was the extensive interview that Alejandro Diago had with Hebe and published in his book, *Hebe de Bonafini: Memoria y esperanza* (Ediciones Dialectica, 1988) that offered solid evidence of Hebe's committed revolutionary evolution.

Jon Lee Anderson's *Che Guevara: A Revolutionary Life* (Grove Press, 1997) gave me insights into Guevara's dream of a Latin American revolution.

An article by Horatio Verbitsky published in October of 2001 in *Pagina 12* seriously forced me to reconsider all of my earlier perceptions of Hebe.

I am also, of course, thankful for Hebe's efforts to bear witness to the horrifying days of the Dirty War as well as for her later writings and speeches that articulate so unmistakably her evolving approach to political change. Her words form important sources for this book.

Most recently, William L. Shirer's *Gandhi: A Memoir* (Pocket Books, 1982) has made me realize the possibilities of true non-violent protest and has led me to reject the idea advanced by Bouvard that the Mothers' movement was "in the Gandhian tradition". There is a greatness of spirit in the person of Gandhi that ultimately seems to be missing in the long and evolving story of Hebe de Bonafini.

I want to thank Luisa López–Grigera, Osvaldo Pardo and Patricia Yocum who read the manuscript in earlier versions and made useful suggestions.

Through all my difficulties in coming to terms with Hebe's political evolution, one person has remained constant for me: my husband, Peter O. Steiner. Most happily, he continues to be my critic, my editor, and still, my greatest friend.

POS
Ann Arbor, Michigan
April 2003

# INTRODUCTION

## The Mothers of the Plaza de Mayo

This book tells the story of the gradual evolution of the Mothers of the Plaza de Mayo, a group of Argentine women whose children were among the estimated 30,000 people who were "disappeared" during the harsh Argentine dictatorship of 1976-1983. These, then middle-aged, mostly uneducated, women with little political savvy are important because, through their effective peaceful protests, they played a significant role in arousing the consciousness of a country that was numbed by silence and paralyzed by fear.

By the downfall of the dictatorship in 1983, the Mothers of the Plaza de Mayo, with their commitment and courage, had become an international symbol of the power of non-violent political action and an inspiration for women's peaceful protest groups around the world. But the story of the Mothers of the Plaza de Mayo does not neatly end there. It continues long after 1983 and the restoration of democracy in Argentina and into the 21st century as the Mothers evolve in new and surprising, even shocking, ways.

## Hebe

The life of the Mothers is inextricably tied to that of a

remarkable woman, Hebe de Bonafini. Born in 1928, she recalls a mostly happy early life in a working-class town south of Buenos Aires. But in 1977 her world was shattered and forever changed by the impact on her family of Argentina's military coup. Her personal experiences have a special relevance because she became the leader of the Mothers of the Plaza de Mayo and has continued as its controversial president into the first years of this century — up to, and beyond, the horrific events of September 11, 2001.

Excerpts from Hebe's personal account of what happened during the course of that evolution are presented here for the first time in English translation and portray the growth of the person she was to become — a rebellious woman of strong opinions and emphatic energy, qualities that have characterized her long and combative life. Her experiences give a face, and a heart, to the disappearance, torture and execution of people during what has become known as Argentina's Dirty War. They provide a first-hand encounter with the circumstances of those times and what it was like to be caught up in their tragic vortex. Her story belies the sense that bad news is conveniently about someone with whom we find it difficult to connect. Or as Hebe expressed it when she was a young mother, and still naive: "our world was a safe fortress. The dead had no names because the story was someone else's."

In 1985, with the help of Matilde Sanchez, Hebe wrote about her life from early childhood until the collapse of the dictatorship in 1983. It is that text which I have translated and edited and is the basis for Part One of this book. Part Two is based on information in the official history of the Mothers of the Plaza de Mayo, written by Hebe and covering the years 1983-1995. Hebe's articles and essays in the monthly publications of the Mothers of the Plaza de Mayo and in their most recent magazine, *Las Locas*, also inform it. Finally, it is based on Hebe's speeches dating from March

23, 1995 to the speech she gave in Buenos Aires soon after the attack on the World Trade Center. Coda I and Coda II reflect my understanding of the status of the Mothers' movement in 1983, after the fall of the dictatorship, and then in 2002 after the attack on the World Trade Center. Throughout the book there are thus two distinct voices. Hebe's, which predominates in Part One, and mine, which plays the leading role in Part Two. They are in different type faces.

This book is not an exhaustive study of Hebe de Bonafini or of the Mothers of the Plaza de Mayo. Rather it provides a valuable first-person testimonial about one person's traumatic experiences during the Dirty War and also a record of the many critical changes that took place in the motivations and activities of the Mothers over the years.

## The Political Background

Argentina's modern political history has been punctuated by instability and a series of military coups. From 1930 to 1976, nine different military juntas overthrew existing governments and attempted to bring order to the country. As one commentator put it: "This spiral of increasingly violent confrontations corresponds neatly with the military's turn toward intolerance and authoritarianism, and with the progressive abandonment of legal or ethical limitations in the methods of repression." [HV-1:170]. During the 1970's, political unrest was intense, with undeclared guerrilla-type warfare between armed groups of both the extreme right and the extreme left.

By this time the always-powerful military had become preoccupied with what they perceived as threats from the enemy within to the values of Western civilization and Christianity. With the strong support of the Catholic Church, the military saw themselves as the elite guardians of "Argentine values" and were convinced that, as their sacred mission, they should purge their country of all "subversive" people. The term "subversive" included not just people involved in overtly violent acts, but, by the military's drastically flexible definition, anyone who challenged or directly opposed what military leaders considered to be the appropriate Argentine way of life. Thus the term "subversive" could embrace trade unionists, intellectuals, teachers, students, lawyers and journalists—as well as people who were merely trying to help the poor in the slums of Buenos Aires.

By November of 1974 the situation during the regime of Isabel Perón had become so chaotic that the government declared a state of siege. More than two hundred people were put in preventive detention. In February 1975 the government created the Argentine Anti-Communist Alliance, the infamous "Triple A", with the goal of completely eradicating "subversive elements". This death squad took immediate action. By the end of 1975 acts of violence had noticeably declined, but the country was still plagued by economic and political instability. Argentina's future seemed extremely precarious.

That future arrived with a resounding vengeance on March 24, 1976 when carefully orchestrated maneuvers by the combined forces of the army, navy and air force overthrew the shaky, but constitutional, government of Isabel Perón. Because the take-over fostered the hope that peace and order would at last be restored to the country, it was a coup that "virtually all Argentines welcomed . . . ." [MF:6] They believed that it was a "gentleman's coup" and, indeed, this belief prompted a supportive reaction by both the international press and the International Monetary Fund which offered the new government substantial loans.

But it was not authentic peace and order that the military restored. Instead, the junta, headed by Army General Jorge Videla, initiated the most brutally repressive regime that the country had known in all of its turbulent 20th century history. While coups and dictatorships, kidnappings

and killings were not new to Argentina, they had never been on the scale of the savage violation of human rights that were to follow during the Dirty War of 1976-1983.

It is the way a group of mothers of the disappeared transformed their grief and frustration into political action that is at the heart of *Hebe's Story*. The evolution of the Mothers after the fall of the dictatorship has hardly been covered in English. It is a story that now needs to be told. It is heartfelt, but nonetheless, extremely troubling. It is a story that serves as a cautionary tale on many counts.

# PART ONE

## HEBE'S STORY AND THE EARLY DAYS OF THE MOTHERS OF THE PLAZA DE MAYO

## CHILDHOOD AND MARRIAGE

# CHAPTER 1

## SNAPSHOTS OF A CHILDHOOD

### *Peaceful Times*

My birth certificate says I was born on December 4, 1928, but I really think I was born on the day I first remember anything. What I recall about my earliest days in El Dique is our small house and the backyard that went down to the dike. There was a henhouse and lots of hens and ducks running around for me to play with. People began to call me by the name they called the chickens. That's where I got my nickname: "Kika". When she was pregnant with me, Mama had studied a list with her friend Conce and had come up with my real name, "Hebe Maria", something entirely exotic for our quiet society.

We had a dog, Full, and he liked to chase after the hens and ducks, but best of all he loved to go hunting with my father and a friend. They'd come back, happy, with partridges or hares.

When my brother was born three years after me, Mama gave him the pompous name of Walmer Herbert Pastor. A few years later, on Saturdays and Sundays when no one on the waterfront was selling sand, he and I would play on the enormous piles of sand that got dumped on the dike. It was our "beach". We used to throw sand at each other or build castles.

When I was very small, my father, Francisco Pastor, used to hoist me up on his shoulders and point to the river. "Look, Kika! Here comes the Pegly—and behind it the Maria." I would watch as the boats and the men slowly became visible through the early morning fog and came closer to our house. At that moment the men on those boats stopped being our neighbors; they were adventurers, rough, fascinating people.

As I grew bigger, I didn't need to get up on my father's shoulders to watch the men coming in from the sea. "Muzzioliii! Muzzioliii!" I'd shout and I'd wave with my handkerchief at the Maria and her brave captain. He'd answer my greeting by waving his Italian cap. Minutes later I'd run into our kitchen to tell Mama that the old captain was coming and to hurry up and get things ready to fix the anchovies— the salt and the small wooden boxes that Papa had made.

Then Muzzioli would tell us in detail just how the anchovies should be filleted so they'd keep for months in the brine. He explained it all as seriously as if he were giving instructions for building a house or performing some medical procedure. Later I was the one who fit those little anchovies into their boxes with the salt. Once in a while my eyes would wander over to the garbage pail where a hundred tiny anchovy heads with their fixed metallic eyes would be peeking out.

We all loved to be around Muzzioli. He told us about different kinds of fish from far away ports, with names that nobody else knew, and about exotic shrimp from Genoa and Naples. He was always gleaming with sweat and a little dirty, but in our eyes those signs of work dignified him. They were proof of his knowledge and authority.

## The Drowned Man

Besides the sailors and the people who worked in the oil refinery in El Dique, there were people who had no homes and who wandered around in rags, solitary, cooking their meals in empty tin cans, protected from the wind by mounds of sand or very high cranes. They didn't steal; in fact, they were like phantoms and we hardly noticed them.

One day my brother came rushing into the house. He just stood there mute, panting with excitement. Then he led me down to the dock and we climbed up on a crane. "Look, Kika," he said. "Now you'll see how they bring out the drowned man."

Everyone had gone down to the dock. My father just looked at what was happening out of the corners of his eyes and seemed to be thinking of something else. My mother refused to look at the spectacle; she put her hands over her eyes. But one way or another everyone in El Dique was there. The whole neighborhood wanted to see the face of the drowned man.

Then what happened, happened. The dead man was brought up hanging by his back on a gigantic hook. "It's the vagabond," somebody shouted. "He must have been drunk and fallen in."

I had seen chickens killed, but with men it was different. We all knew the homeless man well, but now, except for his clothes, he didn't look at all like himself. He had swelled up to double his size and great streams of brown came gushing out of his mouth and nose. Our parents didn't let us see the rest. They just took us by the ears and herded us away from the dock. But all through the next week the drowned man stayed there in my head, swinging from that hook the way meat does in a butcher's shop.

## A Man's World

Who knows how many months our parents must have saved to give my brother and me that green King bicycle. I was nine by then.

"It's all because of you that it's a boys' bike," I said accusingly to my brother. "Don't be stupid, Kika. Don't you see that it makes more sense for you to ride a boys' bike than for me to ride one made for girls? Haven't you figured out yet that it's a man's world. That's the way it is!"

His explanation bothered me. To think he'd use that argument on me. I stayed mad for a few months. And worse, I denied myself the use of the bike until I began to understand that if I didn't ride it, the bike would be only for him. This wasn't the only time that Walmer Herbert Pastor won out.

He and I slept in the same bedroom until I was more than ten years old. Then Papa built a room on the front of the house, a kind of dining room. Once it was finished it became my bedroom. But only at night. During the day it would be used for something else and would stop belonging to me. This didn't seem fair to me either.

## First Rebellion

The only time I remember being sick as a child was when I had asthma. Mama had no idea how to deal with my attacks and so she turned me into a fat little dumpling. "Fat people are healthy people", she said again and again—and I've remained plump for all of my life.

Actually asthma gave me the motive for my first rebellion. "Enough of all these heavy woolen undershirts and poultices and injections, Mama. I've had enough! No more!" I was twelve years old and Mama accepted my decision. Deep down she was just as tired of all this as I was.

## Shattered Dreams

After I finished primary school there wasn't enough money for both my brother and me to study at the lyceum. There wasn't even any family discussion about it—everyone knew that education was for males. The men. They took me out of school.

Too bad, because school had been the most fascinating place on the planet for me. Too bad about me, and my dreams of being a teacher that Sarmiento had inspired. [EN-A: Sarmiento] As a woman, my destiny was to learn to sew. So all I got was a boring, insipid, asphyxiating course in sewing where I pricked my fingers and seemed to do everything wrong.

And the worst of it was that when it was my brother's turn to go to the lyceum, he left of his own accord. "I want to work!" he said—all full of energy—although he hadn't even grown a beard yet. So in our house nobody made it through secondary school.

## Failure

I don't like to do things slowly. I don't like to be quiet. I'm impatient; I'm restless. That business of sewing involved so many steps I just got infuriated.

My sewing teacher, a seamstress in the neighborhood who gave lessons in her home, confronted Mama: "Señora de Pastor, this child isn't learning anything. She disturbs my class, she disobeys. I don't want to throw her out, but this child doesn't have any calling." I was barely 14 years old, but that big to-do about sewing made me proud of myself that I could create such a stir.

Next Mama decided to try my vocation for embroidery. She put me in a class, but it was even worse. Embroidery was just one more failure for me. I embroidered like a monkey.

## The Poncho Business

So then they enrolled me in a weaving class and that, finally, was a success. I liked weaving. It's good because you begin and end quickly.

One night when everyone was asleep, I began to do some wash. As I was washing, I began to draw pictures in my head. First a little jacket, then a little shawl and later a poncho. I went on with my soaping and there came to me the idea of a shawl–like poncho and then afterwards, a poncho–like shawl with a belt. I ended up drying my hands and drawing sketches. Maybe I was on to something–at last.

"You could really do something with those ponchos," my friend, Queca, said. "I think you could make some beautiful things. You should make things you can sell."

And I did. One hundred little ponchos–what madness! My maiden aunt, Clara, and Rosa, Rosita and Dora all came into the poncho business with me. We bought a sewing machine and that speeded up the work; we turned out little jackets and hats like hot cakes.

Before long our ponchos saturated the market and we began selling them in other cities. When I walked around in La Plata I would see people wearing my ponchos. "Pardon me, Señora, but where did you buy that poncho?" "Ah," the woman would answer proudly "this is a Cordoba poncho. Everyone's wearing them there."

## Politics in El Dique

As I got older I saw that our world was divided in two: the workers and the merchants. Each group had its own club: the United Club and the bigger Mariano Moreno Club that had an auditorium where candidates would launch their local campaigns. [EN-B: Moreno]

For our family, everything centered on the club. It was our society. We belonged to the United Club that brought together the workers from the hat factory, where Papa worked, the oil refinery and other factories in our neighborhood. The men played soccer together and had bocci teams. They even built duplexes for each other and they plastered walls and painted bathrooms together. Eventually the workers gave our club a small library with modern novels and a few technical books on mechanics and construction. Through their combined efforts, they were working to improve their community.

But theirs was a light-hearted approach. People in El Dique had the strange capacity for transforming more serious things, such as politics or catastrophes, into social events. Before each election the two clubs vied with each other in their street paintings. That, of course, meant a fiesta. Politics, in fact, seemed to be nothing more than festive rivalries between the two political sides in the surrounding ten blocks.

## Women

And where were the women while all the men were painting in the streets? They were in the clubhouse, glued to the radio, getting the dinner that their husbands would eat when they got back from painting. Some of the women were enthusiastic radicals, others strongly supported the Peronists. The only way they worked for their parties was by cooking those dinners that everyone enjoyed.

The truly militant women invariably belonged to the Communist Party. These women were different, sure of themselves, frightfully independent. They worked for the neighborhood, they offered their opinions. We knew them well and yet they seemed to want to keep their distance. We respected them, but we wanted to keep our distance too.

For us, a woman's intelligence was measured by the variety of ideas she could translate into ways of saving money. The idea of "family progress" was the principle that made us think that "saving is the basis for a fortune". Peso after peso and hour after hour, our family worked to bring us closer to that goal. My mother, Josefa Boguetti, kept track of our daily savings in her notebook. We felt obliged to save all year to off-set that wretched month of forced vacation when the hat factory closed and Papa didn't get any salary.

There wasn't enough money to buy notebooks so my mother patiently saved the brown paper the butcher used for wrapping chickens. Then she'd say, "Kika, use a good sharp pencil and make nice straight lines and don't be in too much of a hurry." But first she folded the pieces of paper in half and bound them together with a few stitches.

I filled my homemade notebooks with clippings about those famous men, Moreno and Sarmiento, and I also made a meticulous collection of pressed leaves. Trees enchant me. I can spend hours just looking at them. They have a sense of harmony and are one of the few things that can soothe me.

## Dances

When I was a little older, another aunt, an "old maid" of about 30, used to take me to dances at the United Club. All the women wore long dresses. There was an orchestra; I learned to dance—tangos, tarantelas, pasadobles, the milonga. In winter it was cold in our little clubhouse and in summer we about died of the heat. But it was exciting. By one in the morning at a dance in the summer, half the neckties would have been tossed aside, the dresses full of wrinkles, the sequined hems turned black and our fancy hairdos drooping.

One time when we were in Buenos Aires visiting Aunt Juanita and Uncle Natalio, we realized that everyone didn't see our dances the way we did. Maybe it was without thinking, I don't know, but my aunt suddenly blurted out, "How ignorant people are! So poor and yet they wear long dresses to go to a dance in a simple shed."

Mama turned pale and looked at me. She put on a false smile and just went on talking. Aunt Juanita and Uncle Natalio were family but they lived in Buenos Aires. Once in a while, on week-ends, they'd come down to El Dique and our family would make a big fuss over having a barbecue for them. And now Aunt Juanita came out with that. Mama pretended that it didn't matter—but she was mortally wounded.

## Papa

My brother and I complained that Papa was just wearing himself out for nothing, but Papa never complained. From morning until night he worked in the factory making hats by hand. My friend, Queca, whose father was the boss at the hat factory, told me that people said that he could turn out more hats in an hour than anyone else.

In his spare time Papa built a small house in the backyard, "in case the grandparents might need it some day". But he was also concerned with problems in the neighborhood. He was a liberal (all El Dique was liberal) but it wasn't a very fervent liberalism. His most important connections were with the directors of the club or the school.

When my father bought a radio after some years it was a real event, not only in our house, but in the whole neighborhood. The night he brought it home nobody slept; we tried all the stations in collective sessions of radio theater. Later, while we listened, we also learned how to cross-stitch, and how to make the dough for doughnuts.

All Papa expected in life were simple things, small gratifications—the children growing up without problems, being able to take a trip to Salta some day—things like that. And what did he hope for in the outside world?—That his club would prosper, that the hunting would be good and that the next year he'd have a better tomato crop.

## A Happy Routine

In our lives of limited variety, there was an acceptance that we should look for pleasure in our work and that we should always try to add some kind of work to our pleasure. That attitude was authentic and deeply felt.

Above everything else El Dique was a happy place. In the morning the houses would be opened wide, whether it was hot or cold. The women aired them, singing as they did the cleaning, always singing tangos or humming sambas or bullfight music. For my grandmother, whistling was almost as natural as breathing. We didn't have any time-saving machines. Singing was the way to work and amuse yourself at the same time. Singing, the clothes were washed on the washboard, and then left for hours on the grass in the sun until they became white. Then they were washed again. The process took all day. One looked closely for spots, like a detective. (Did we perhaps stretch out these activities to make them seem more important?)

The simplest things were transformed into great family projects—both to save money and because it gave us that sense of pleasant usefulness. Everything, even soap, was made by hand. From Berisso and from La Plata, where the rest of our family lived, the relatives would arrive, the aunts and uncles and the grandparents, all laden with packages. One brought pots, another had fat and potash. My father made little soap boxes out of discarded wood. Then on some sunny day, in the backyard, the firewood and the stew pot would produce the miraculous, nauseating paste that, after hours of smoking, would harden into soap.

The same thing happened on "salsa day". Dozens of

tomatoes, onions, garlic, cloves and spices were stirred around in the great cauldron in our backyard. The house would be filled with that acid aroma of the pulp. Later everyone put it into bottles for the rest of the year.

## Reflection

Looking back today, the world of El Dique seems transparent and uninteresting. We didn't know then what lay in wait for us. We lived in our own little world, run by its own rules and far, far away from the capital. Our small group, made up of relatives, friends and neighbors, seemed somehow to be a prisoner of its own ordinariness.

Outside of this tight circle nothing looked too important. It was another country and as remote as some foreign capital. Buenos Aires was the seat of "national institutions", the residence of the President and his ministers, the place where serious health problems were resolved, or, once in a long while, where you said good-bye to someone who was going on a trip. The rest of the time we lived with our backs to Buenos Aires. It was something that had nothing to do with us, a place we weren't able to handle.

So time stretched out for us, always the same. Every day was similar to the one before and I even believe that there existed a pleasure in seeing it repeat itself. But, truthfully, we really looked forward to those simple exciting events that broke into our usual, peaceful routine.

# CHAPTER 2

## MARRIAGE AND MOTHERHOOD

*Toto*

"That man has an irresistible attraction," I confided to Queca. "Do you think that . . . ?"

"But, of course, Kika. He can't take his eyes off you. If he comes over to you, look at him a little—like this . . . . Just use your judgment, okay? But don't run away from him!"

I began to water the plants at the worst time of day, in the heat of the midday sun, just so I could catch a glimpse of him on his way back from lunch at the restaurant nearby. I knew his name was Humberto but that people called him Toto. I never talked with him very much, but I knew I liked him. Our glances met one afternoon and after that he began to wait for me at the corner.

Right away my maiden aunt caught us meeting and said that at fourteen I shouldn't be thinking about pants. "And," she added "he can't be more than sixteen if he's just beginning to have the shadow of a beard. But if you like him . . . ." I went right on watering the plants.

One afternoon Toto came up to me on his way home from work. He started to talk right away: "The truth is, really, I want to say something, really, because I, I feel attracted. If you're not adverse—and it doesn't seem so. But I don't want to make a secret of it. If I have to, I'll proclaim it quite formally. My intentions are serious . . . ." The lemon tree had become drowned in water. I shut off the faucet and told him that I'd think about it.

"Oh, Kika, how exciting!" Queca said and she suggested that I tell Mama about it. So I told Mama, and she told Papa, and he came to me and said, very dryly, that before we went out walking together in the neighborhood Humberto could visit me at home on Thursdays. Toto began visiting me in the afternoon.

We had mate (tea) together and we talked about the club, about the Capitaneo and Pesado families that were building duplex houses, about the ponchos I was making and about dances that were being planned.

Finally, after six years of courtship, we began to make plans to get married. Years ago my father had built a little house of sheet metal in the backyard and he told us we could live there after we got married. We didn't have much of a social life, except for parties at the club, so we could put all our energy and savings into getting the house set up. We didn't waste even 40 centavos on going to the movies. Best of all, the ponchos were selling well—many as far away as Cordoba.

Toto and I got engaged in 1949 on a rainy afternoon in the midst of a thunder and lightening storm. "Luck for the fiancée!" proclaimed the excited aunts and one of the relatives who'd had a little too much vermouth. And, indeed, a little while later Toto commented on how fortunate we were.

"Just look at our luck, Hebe!" Toto exclaimed. "Everything is working out. Your father is going to let us use the backyard house. And now we have a little gas oven and we can get a second-hand ice box cheap. What more could we need? We even have a thousand pesos left over to splurge like kings on a month in La Falda. Time, nothing more, is all we need."

The girls who worked with me at home on the ponchos and my friends from the weaving class gave me a "farewell" party one evening at the Paris de La Plata tearoom—a luxury. I made myself a green dress for the occasion and afterwards we went to the mass that the nuns put on for me in the shabby annex of the Miscericordia Church.

For the civil marriage I wore a blue suit with a gray blouse that Rosita Rubio made for me. With Toto dressed in the same color, we looked like something out of a fashion magazine. Afterwards we had a party—little sandwiches and cider, music and dancing. Queca, Pin, Haydee, Orfilia, and Pochi were all there. "Oh, Toto, I'm so happy!"

Then, on November 12th, 1949, Toto and I were formally married in the Church of San Francisco in La Plata. I was finally calling myself Hebe Pastor de Bonafini.

The girls who still weren't married were all waiting for me to get back from my honeymoon so I could tell them about everything. The wedding night is as it should be, a time when all mysteries are dissolved and everything that happens is complete with all the truths and distortions that our imaginations have created a thousand and one times. The problem was to know which was more beautiful—what I had just experienced or what I had dreamed about for so long.

## Jorge is Born

On the 10th of December, 1950, I am in the Italian Hospital of La Plata. I hurt all over and they have warned me that this is going to be "a long one". But I am happy. I am going to be a mother. Dios mio! I'm dying of curiosity to see how it will be. Humberto is beside me. In reality, the whole country is here with me. My room has been invaded by uncles and aunts, cousins, friends and neighbors in one big festive party.

Finally only Toto and Mama are with me. All during my two days of labor Mama keeps rearranging the suitcase full of baby clothes. All those little gowns and booties—105 booties and 45 gowns. They gave me a ball of yarn and I just got busy. I must never have slept the whole nine months.

In the delivery room everything speeds up and there's a confusion of orders and finally the scream and, right afterwards, the awaited cry. "A boy, healthy and strong," says Dr. Chescota.

At that moment I am filled with a tremendous flood of words. I begin to talk to the nurses about all kinds of things—that they should dress the baby in the striped yellow outfit, that he's going to be called Jorge, that they should show him to Toto before they bathe him. And I think to myself "You were born, my baby, on the 12th of December, 1950 at twenty after one in the morning, and I am your mother."

When we get home Toto carries the baby into the house. Toto lets his little face peek out between the covers and says to him, "When you begin to see things, you'll know the Maria and you're going to walk along the dikes. And this is your wash room and this is your kitchen where you'll eat with us and this is where Papa will put you to soak up the sun."

No doubt about it. Things were working out just as we'd dreamed. We were so happy in that little warm house with a view of the river. I was a contented woman. And I was in love with that man who knew how to bathe his son, who every day came home a little earlier.

## Wet Nurse

"I don't know if you'd be able to . . .", said the woman. She was a good neighbor whom we had known for years through the club. She didn't quite know how to ask me that favor, but she finally said. "I don't have any milk and the milk you buy is never the same." "No," I said "of course the milk is not the same."

I always had a lot of milk and I was going to take Jorge off the breast soon. So I accepted. I told the woman that she should bring her son Daniel to me on schedule, every day. Then I would nurse the two boys, one after the other.

Something wonderful happened to me when I held both of them, as they grabbed onto my breast like two little chiggers. To put a baby to my breast was, in a certain sense, to prolong the pregnancy, to keep up that chain of activity based on necessity. To give them food was to give them freedom, but it also meant that I was renouncing my own freedom. Haydee would invite me to the theater, Queca would insist that I go to the movies, but I preferred to stay at home where there was the best that life had to offer.

## Happy Times

After Jorge was born, Mama and I began to make dustcoats by the dozens in the afternoon. We didn't make a fortune, but it helped. Mama had bought an electric refrigerator where I kept our food. We weren't materialistic so I didn't want Humberto to work overtime. I really longed to have more children, and to have time for us to stroll along the dikes together—to be a good close family and to watch our children grow up happily. Everything was going smoothly. Jorge turned one year old without getting a single cold. So happy we were. But what was going to happen to us?

"Put that fear of yours out of your head, Kika. There are people where nothing ever happens." "Yes, yes, I know," I answered. But at night I would think that I would rather have had a few small setbacks like everyone else, at least to have something to complain about.

When Jorge was two, I was thrilled to be pregnant

again. This time we said that everything was going to be more in control. "A modern birth, Toto, not like some big party at the club." And that's the way it was.

I had another boy—Raúl.

"Ah, Kika, another little boy. Now we can dress them alike . . .", smiled Toto, trying to hide his disappointment in not having a girl. I had made a little rose-colored ruffled outfit for the new baby, but in just a few days it was entirely forgotten. Raúl was the picture of his father. Out in the backyard there was a steady stream of diapers hanging on the line. The house filled up with baby smells and the sound of the laughter of Jorge and his little friends. Everything was very happy.

Humberto didn't want to lose any of that happiness so to get to work faster, he bought a used, black bicycle from old Constantini. "We'll put a light on it," we told each other. "But we'll have to wait until next month." To buy that headlight, to get the money.

He would put the bike on the train to La Plata, get off and then pedal the 30 blocks to the oil refinery. It saved time and carfare. That saving, just as my grandparents had done, as my own parents had done, was transformed into a small bit of progress. One tiny step of progress.

And what happened to me? Nothing. Toto was right. I shouldn't be so full of fears. Anyway, life was interesting and I was content and completely focused on my home and family. I was perfectly happy just to stay at home with my boys.

Then one night Toto came home, all bubbling over, and announced to me that I should get ready to go out and give my 29th birthday a proper celebration. "We're going to celebrate it on Corrientes Street in Buenos Aires." I thought it was a wonderful idea. A month would not be any too much time to get ready for such an event. At 29 I had only traveled to the capital twice. I got our tin of savings and took out a few pesos.

In Buenos Aires, that night in December, we had dinner and then went to the theater to see a play where they made jokes about "a deposed tyrant." I didn't like it and I certainly didn't understand what they were talking about. They told jokes about Congress and mentioned names that didn't mean anything to me. It would be years before I had any desire to visit Buenos Aires again.

By Hebe's frank admission what was happening in Buenos Aires and the rest of the country hardly affected her. When Perón's dictatorship came to a bloody end in 1955, hundreds of his followers were killed in a bombing at the Plaza de Mayo. The years 1955 and 1956, during the brief military regime of Pedro Aramburu, were ones of severe repression for Perónism. It was a time of revolutions and rebellions—of executions and a horrifying massacre of Perónist sympathizers. [EN-C: *Operación Masacre*] This unrest quite definitely registered in El Dique, although Hebe confessed that it didn't make much of an impression on her.

For me, life went on as always. All the awful things that were happening in the outside world seemed very impersonal—and as irremediable as a meteorological catastrophe. Indeed, for us women, the news on the radio, no matter how drastic, didn't succeed in drowning out the sound of washing the dishes or the almost incessant bubbling up of some casserole. Our heads were always somewhere else.

In this way our world was a safe fortress. The dead had no names because the story was someone else's. There was in us a numbness, an insensibility, because our emotional response was reduced to that small circle of family and neighbors. Our world was limited by the certainty that we would be happy, because happiness is written in small letters and is expressed slowly, with modesty, in small acts. And, anyway, what could we do about the killings and barbarity that had become a background to our lives? The individual seemed completely helpless and unable to change anything.

## The Boys Grow Up

By the time Jorge was ten he was reading a lot. I thought of him as a little intellectual. He took books out of the library at the club and he'd study, very seriously, at his table. He seemed to be off in his own world.

Raúl, in contrast, was the observing kind, incapable of concentrating on anything but his adventures. He liked to spend his time outdoors, on his hands and knees in ditches, looking at insects or the trees, studying the comings and going of spiders and ants. He would put insects in bottles with chloroform and look at their legs through a magnifying glass. And, as presents, he would ask for books with photographs of insects.

About this time, Humberto got involved in constructing a puppet theater. Mama and I made the puppets, Jorge wrote the scripts, and with the help of three or four retired people from the neighborhood, he began to give performances in our living room. (For seats, we borrowed metal chairs from the club.) The puppet theater made Jorge the king of the neighborhood.

We built Raúl a tree house in the paradise tree in the backyard. High in the branches, Raúl would organize races between his teams of ants, and Jorge would sit there and read. When he was about nine, Raúl wrote me a poem for Mother's Day. It was just a childish thing, expressing his love for me, but I thought it was the most marvelous thing in the world.

Our sons were growing up. Each new step they took filled

me with euphoria and suggested new mysteries. They were "my sons", with all the strength that those two words could possibly have. But they were also individuals. Each of them had his own personality, his own disposition. I soon realized that to be a good mother meant knowing exactly when I should let them go their own ways. But there would always be an indissoluble bond between us. We were united forever.

I didn't have the feeling that I was just some ordinary, mediocre person with an almost vulgar destiny. My sons were making me feel different. Like a unique, irreplaceable person. They were, no doubt about it, a creation of mine, a kind of legacy, my contribution to the world, to history, to life. I, Hebe Pastor, had added to the world something that had never before existed. Who knows, they might become important human beings or simply "good people". In the future. I am not ashamed to say that my sons were my justification for being.

## Political Unrest

In 1965, Hebe's family grew to five with the birth of Alejandra. Finally there was a girl and they all adored her. Although things were going along happily at home, on the political scene trouble was definitely brewing.

That year a bomb exploded at the state gas company. The explosions lasted all afternoon and stirred up the river like a sea of muddy water. All of us rushed out of our houses that cold winter day, carrying only what seemed most valuable—shivering children, tin cans with our monthly savings or, even, the fruit we'd just put up in jars. Our own family, I with our new baby, went flying off to our cousin's house in La Plata. There we would stay listening to the radio until we heard that it was safe to go back home.

In the meantime some radio announcer would talk about what he'd just seen—burning pieces of wood tearing through the air, flames flaring up around houses near ours, oil depots that could burn and take all of El Dique with them. All this was going on while people everywhere in town were running away from the frightful scene.

Although El Dique had been a place free from political struggle until then, there were now factions that were trying to stir up political trouble with acts of sabotage. Our house, because it was near the oil refinery and the gas company, and not far from the infantry installation and the naval hospital, was caught in the crossfire.

Before any military incident, and even before any warning on the radio of some "surprise" attack, the police would knock on our door to alert us, "There's a bomb at the refinery. Get out of here right away!" And we'd have to leave home, just as we were. It was like that before every incident.

Nobody ever asked who had set the bombs; the names of those people never appeared in the papers. Nobody wondered what right anyone had to bomb anything and to make trouble in the middle of the night and up-end our lives. We had to evacuate and that was the end of it. No questions asked.

## High School Years

And then before I realized it, Jorge and Raúl had become young men and were in high school at the prestigious National College. They were really studying now. Jorge took part in the student theater group and Raúl kept right on bottling insects. They were growing up; their voices were becoming deeper.

As they became older I observed them quietly, from a certain distance. Fortunately I never found it necessary to be a watchdog over them. But I kept right on worrying though Toto always tried to calm me. "You see, Kika, everything's going fine for our family, almost perfectly. Some day the boys are going to be professionals, and good professionals, each in his own field. And they're going to love their work."

"But so much good fortune, Humberto. What's going to happen to us?"

One morning Raúl asked me in a reproving tone "Mama, how do you read the newspaper?". I was standing at the living room table where at that moment I was leafing through the paper. In reply I just put my hands up in the air as if I had no answer. "Well, first I read the comics, then the death notices and the crime page."

"Oh, Mama, you're all mixed up. Our history professor taught us the right way to read the paper. First, the national news, then the international reports and, only then, if there's time, all the rest."

The newspaper had always seemed boring to me, but perhaps with Raúl's help I might give it a chance. I felt more and more that I should give my children the opportunity to teach me things. I sensed that I had a whole world to learn. Raúl stood beside me and turned to the national news.

I glanced at him. "You won't believe it, but I don't understand these news stories. I begin to read and I get lost. Newspapers don't talk the way we do."

Raúl laughed and said that they would never speak the way we do, but that I had to learn to understand what they were saying. "You can't be ignorant of those things, Mama. I'm going to teach you."

From that morning on we read the newspaper together. Raúl explained the words I didn't understand and the most complicated sentences. And he taught me to read between the lines.

One morning the boys tore into the dining room like a couple of wild Indians. "Happy birthday!" Jorge gave me a big hug; Raúl spun me around in the air. Then Jorge gave me something he had hidden behind his back—a book.

*Bomarzo* by Manuel Mujica Lainez. I was speechless. No one had given me a book in a long, long time. I felt so happy that Jorge wanted to share with me the secret pleasure of reading.

That very afternoon I gave it a try. I struggled for four hours with a great stew of unknown words. I was about ready to cry. I wondered if I'd ever be able to read books. When I told Jorge about the trouble I was having, he sat me down and made me read with him. "All right, Jorge. Here, for example is someone who seems to be important, but I don't know who he is—Miguel Angel Buonarotti . . . ."

"That's Michelangelo, a famous painter and sculptor who . . . ."

"But, wait. Here it speaks about the *Iliad*—what is the *Iliad*? Then it says something about 'the chess game of life'. You can see how hard all this is for me."

"What you have to do is read with a dictionary beside you. If you don't understand something, look it up. That's how you'll learn."

I thought about all the things that Jorge knew. Good gracious, how I wished I'd been born in the 50's like him so I'd be part of that different, open world that he enjoyed so much. But, anyway, Jorge didn't think of me as an "ignoramus". "Don't worry Mama. You know other things—things that you've learned because you've lived them. These things will help you when you need them."

Months later Jorge gave me another book. For this one you don't need a dictionary or a history book or anything. It was a book of poetry by Pablo Neruda. Jorge had me read a little out loud. He said I'd understand it—that I should just let my mind run free, like I do with music. He talked about how poetry uses symbols and then he began to explain Neruda's poetry to me. I wished that he would never finish with his explanations, that he would just stay there with me, telling me the whole book and then another one, with that nearness and warmth, with that return of love that I gave him when he was a little boy. While he was reading, Neruda's poetry was absolutely clear to me.

My love for my sons had gradually become another kind of love without my realizing it. By the time I became conscious of it, there had already grown between Raúl, Jorge and me a feeling of respect. Perhaps for me it was a less powerful or tangible love than when they were little, but it certainly was more mature.

Now my sons were nurturing me. It was like seeing things for the first time, like being born anew. And in many ways that is just what it was; my sons had given me a second birth—and this time not in innocence.

I also challenged them. I wanted to be less "mother" and more "companion", to let them encourage me with their thoughts, their endless energy, their youth that was always doing something. They breathed life into every particle of my being that was trying to push outward into the world, attempting to shake off my lazy habits. They wanted me to study, to be a good reader, to use my time for something worthwhile—even if it was for no more purpose than just reading the newspaper. With Jorge and Raúl as my teachers, all my fears about being ridiculed faded away.

## Coming of Age Politically

Then gradually, without any loud insistence or strong declarations, but simply by the way they behaved and thought, Jorge and Raúl began to question Toto's and my fixed ideas. They often discussed the political situation, they criticized the world that we had constructed, they demolished our reasons, they shot down the sure, safe beliefs of our generation. [Both Jorge and Raúl would have been thoroughly familiar with the writings of the Argentine guerrilla hero, Ernesto "Che" Guevara (1928-1967) who with Fidel Castro in 1959 overthrew the Cuban dictatorship of Fulgencio Batista.] [EN-D: "Che" Guevara]

The boys' early rebelliousness was not without reason; I could see that some of what they felt was justified or at least open to serious question. There were dark, shameful corners in that world that we had left for them. Toto and I represented past history and the boys were able to see the political mistakes that had been made by people of our generation. Our sons were our most important judges.

They sought a rendering of accounts from us and challenged us to look with new eyes at things that were happening in our country. They were much more reflective and thoughtful than we had been as young people—or even as adults. They didn't necessarily accept the way things were. They felt that established truths should always be subject to examination.

For example, one cold rainy day a boy in the neighborhood came to us asking for some old clothes. Jorge, who was about sixteen, turned to me and asked, "Mama, what should we give him?"

And I answered, "If we have more than we need, then we should give it to someone who really needs it."

"No. Mama, you're wrong," Jorge replied. "We must share the little that we have."

During the heyday of the hippies, the boys focused twice as hard on their studies. But they also felt very deeply about what was happening in the world around them and about their own ideas of what should be done to change that world.

At school they joined clubs that had heated discussions about Argentine history. For me history jumped from Independence in 1810 to Sarmiento's presidency later in the century. I was indifferent to it all. But my sons talked about history with the passion of the present. They discussed it backwards and forwards and debated who had been our greatest heroes. I saw them as adolescents in a marvelous stage of discovery. They were preoccupied with the future; they were involved. And they realized that they each had a role to play.

## Changes

Soon the boys stopped being just adolescents and became serious students. Jorge was one of the best physics students at the University of La Plata and became a teaching assistant in mathematics and physics. Later he also worked with the priest Federico Bachini (now disappeared) who recruited university students to volunteer in poor neighborhoods to teach adults to read.

Meanwhile, Raúl, the lively, good-looking joker, had decided to give free rein to his passion for insects and was studying natural science and also working as a laborer and a minor official for his trade union.

By then Jorge had a serious girl friend, Maria Elena Bugnone, who taught Spanish. They were always at the house. They liked my pies, my "speciality" (chicken with olives), they wore pullovers I knit for them, and they often woke us up at two in the morning when they came back to the house with friends for coffee. I loved having students around because it filled the house with life and they were always focused on the future.

Then, quite suddenly, something new happened. Jorge and Raúl both became militant. "Don't be afraid of that word or reject it, Mama. To be militant is to be concerned; it's the same thing that grandfather did in the neighborhood and at the club. It's trying to help other people to have better lives. And to be militant has nothing to do with soldiers. Don't worry, Mama."

# CHAPTER 3

## HITTING HOME

### Introduction: The 1976 Coup

During the years that Jorge and Raúl were growing up there were almost constant undercurrents of political unrest. They were years of fierce labor strikes and turmoil in the universities. Violence—kidnappings, assassinations, massacres and guerrilla warfare—became an unnerving presence on Argentina's political scene. But with the coup of March 24, 1976, political repression entered a new, even more terrifying, stage.

Immediately after the junta took power, it enacted a severely repressive plan, the so-called Process for National Reorganization, which gave it the legal right to commit all manner of atrocities. The excuse for this action was that it had become necessary in order to suppress terrorism and restore order to Argentina.

Within hours of the coup, Congress was dissolved. Members of the Supreme Court were replaced by men who supported the military government. Political and trade union activity were prohibited. Control of universities was taken over by the military. Censorship was imposed and strictly enforced. In effect, all civil rights were suspended.

People were detained. A great many of them disappeared altogether and were never seen again. Men and women, even teen-agers, were abducted from their homes, kidnapped on the streets or at their places of work or study. Once detained, they had no legal recourse, no lawyers and no trials.

The number of "disappeared" grew painfully through 1977. Detention centers, 340 in all, were set up in a variety of buildings previously used for other purposes—police stations, schools, factories, military barracks, a motel, an athletic club. The most notorious of these was the Naval Mechanics School (ESMA), located right in the fashionable heart of Buenos Aires. Stories circulated about detention centers that specialized in relentless, degrading tortures. There were reports of clandestine executions. Mutilated bodies began to wash up on the shores of the River Plate.

Often prisoners were mercilessly tortured, both physically and psychologically, so that they would become disoriented, lose all sense of their identity as human beings and eventually "break"—perhaps divulging some information or occasionally becoming collaborators in helping to round up other "subversives". Hundreds of people died during this relentless abuse; others were able to endure the most grueling tortures without totally collapsing. But their endurance did not save them; almost always they were "transferred" to their certain deaths. The familiar sequence was abduction, prison, torture, death. [EN-E: Torture]

Fear shaped the pattern of everyday life in Argentina. Most lawyers were afraid to file writs of habeas corpus— afraid that they too, or their families, might become victims. The Catholic Church, in keeping with its long history of standing behind the military, was generally supportive of the regime and was of little help to families of the disappeared.

Another cause for the looming sense of fear was the government's attempt to suppress the Argentine people by keeping them completely in the dark. The junta denied everything that was happening and on the day of the coup issued a decree that anyone who did anything or published anything that might be damaging to the Armed Forces, security officials or the police would be imprisoned for ten years. Specific decrees were put into action that took a number of politically influential newspapers out of circulation. In this way, with insinuation, threats and actual coercion, the junta intimidated the press and effectively limited the normal avenues for disseminating information. Most people, out of fright and the paucity of reliable information, slipped into a helpless silence. [EN-F: Media]

Finally, by November of 1976, the violation of human rights became so blatant that Amnesty International came to Argentina to investigate. Its report indicated that it did not accept the junta's justification that such actions were necessary to preserve freedom and justice in the country. Rather, Amnesty International concluded that the military government had undermined individual liberty and seriously threatened justice by suspending fundamental constitutional rights and guarantees. It reported that the police had been given absolute power to arrest and detain and that the military junta had been exempted from any legal responsibility for the disappearances and deaths of innocent people. It bluntly described the situation in Argentina as "alarming". [EN-G: Amnesty International]

Marguerite Feitlowitz in her remarkable book, A Lexicon of Terror, tells about the impact of the coup on La Plata. " . . . in terms of education, intellectual life, and social movements, La Plata has been historically avant-garde. Its Museum of Natural Sciences is the best in South America". Students from all over Argentina, indeed the continent, were attracted by the vigor and the engaged political profile of the National University of La Plata. "Logically enough, La Plata was a special target of the repression. Proportionally it lost more of its younger population (16-27 year olds) than any other Argentine city." [MF:178]

Throughout 1975 and 1976, life in La Plata was constantly interrupted by gunshots and kidnappings. University students began to go into hiding; many were disappeared. On the night of September 16, 1976, seven high-school students were kidnapped from their homes because of their role in lobbying for lower bus fares. This tragic event is remembered now as "The Night of the Pencils", in an ironic twist of "The Night of the Long Knives" of the Nazi Third Reich.

Hebe has written very little about the political scene in Argentina in the 1970's or the catastrophic year of 1976. But even her meager entries suggest her sense of foreboding. She soon felt its repercussions.

## Early Warnings

Army trucks began coming down El Camino General Belgrano in front of our new house in City Bell, a suburb of La Plata. We could see them out of our windows. Each time the soldiers came even closer, each time they were more forceful, more dangerous. They started walking on the sidewalk out in front, then coming into our kitchen, then sitting down at the table, and finally going into our bedrooms and looking under our beds. They recorded our conversations.

One time, a little later, when Jorge was at our new house, we had mate together and he did a lot of talking. He spoke about Maria Elena, to whom he was married by then, and about the last chapter of his dissertation on the laser.

Then he talked about what was happening at the university, about friends and professors who had been detained (that was the word that the groups who worked to free political prisoners used in 1976). "But it's different,

Mama, because they're like clandestine prisoners. Nobody can bring them clothes or food; nobody can even see them."

I told him again that he should be careful, especially now that he was about to graduate. All I was afraid of was that they might reject his monograph.

On January 1, 1977, after our New Year's party, I had a serious conversation with Jorge.

"Jorge, look at me, listen to me carefully. Wouldn't it be wiser if you went away for a few months? Any place—to your uncle's, or to the hotel in San Clemente where we used to go in the summer. You know that they're taking away your friends, your professors. And, as you say they're nothing more than dissidents. Just go off for a month. Wherever you want to go—until they let up with all their arrests.

"Maria Elena is hardly a month pregnant. What would it hurt her to wait for you a little while? And if she doesn't want to stay at home, she can go with you. All this worries me. How can you go on being so calm, knowing that the president of the university, that "rooster" as you say, lives by marking students—the ones who write petitions or hand out flyers?

"Jorge, I know all about how you're only a month away from finishing your studies, that you almost have your dissertation written and that you have friends who are prisoners and that you would feel badly to go away.

"I know all that. And I also know that you're no longer a baby and I can't make you do anything, but yes, you are a child. You're scarcely twenty-seven years old, a young kid with not much experience. Please!"

By February of 1977, Jorge was more concerned than ever about my brother who had been sick for a long time and was dying. Jorge often went to see him in the hospital. But I told him, "Don't worry so much about your friends and your uncle, Jorge. Finish your monograph."

The next time Jorge went to the hospital to visit my brother he telephoned me right afterwards.

"Mama, it's me!" he shouted. He was talking from a public telephone. The honking of horns and the noise of all the traffic made it hard to talk. "I'm going to talk with your parents, Mama. Can you hear me? I think that they'll take it better if I tell them the bad news about your brother."

I listened and I felt proud. I thought how lucky Toto and I were to have two sons who were such good people—and to have Alejandra as well. I went on listening, thankful that Jorge was going to save me the sad business of telling my parents that their son was dying.

"I'm going back home now to have lunch, Mama. Then I'll go to El Dique and talk with the grandparents. All right?"

With so much noise, I could hardly hear Jorge. I thought about how he'd be going to the house by the dikes where I grew up, where my mother and father and his uncle lived, where we had been a happy family. I felt relieved.

"Thanks, Jorge," I answered and I hung up. That would be our last conversation.

## Disappearance

This is the way Hebe imagined what happened to Jorge from everything that she learned later.

. . . five cars pull up to the door. Green, red, and white Torinos. Goons with heavy weapons in each car, swarms of them.

It's so hot at ten in the morning that a few men from the neighborhood are sitting out by the street, enjoying the last minutes of fresh air. When the cars drive up and screech to a stop, the onlookers are fascinated. But they're also afraid. They retreat into their houses.

The goons shoot off the lock on Jorge's front door. There's no one inside so they decide to wait. They're in no hurry.

They turn on the radio, sit down and put their feet up on the table.

Jorge arrives at noon. He doesn't have much time to have lunch before leaving for El Dique. He hasn't noticed the five cars at the door. He doesn't realize that he should turn around and get out of there fast. Instead he's thinking about his uncle as he pushes open the door. That's when he gets the first blow.

He gets up. The pain is as bad as his surprise. He looks at them; there are ten of them now and he sees that they've broken some of the furniture. Just as he realizes they're in civilian clothes, they hit him again and then a third time. After that there's only one long, monotonous, drawn-out blow.

A neighbor hears the screams and turns on the radio so the goons won't know that he's heard what's going on. They keep on beating Jorge. When they finally carry him out the door, the neighbors don't look out their windows.

Maria Elena finishes her classes at seven that evening. She buys something for dinner at the deli and goes home. As she approaches the house she sees the door, but she goes in.

Disaster. Broken furniture, books torn up and thrown every which way—and studded clubs. On top of all this, as the most powerful demonstration of the junta's repugnant power, Jorge's monograph on the laser has been reduced to tiny pieces of paper. Maria Elena throws down her package and frantically looks for Jorge—but she knows he's not there. She leaves everything just as it is and comes looking for me.

Together we go to the university and then to a friend's house. "I don't know if they only broke into the house or if they took him away," Maria Elena cries. She is desperate. It is midnight and there is no one to ask now. And besides, who would have the courage to go and ask the neighbors? Heaven knows, maybe those goons are still around.

Finally, by phone, we reach the grocer on the corner, a good man. At five in the morning he answers our call and says, "Yes, they took him away. He was unconscious and they threw him into the Ford Torino like a sack of meal." We hang up. Now we know—but what are we going to do?

## Search

During that interminable week in February of 1977 I believe we didn't even sleep, that we were getting in and out of the car all the time, endlessly, without thinking about anything, and about everything, all at the same time.

I have tried to retrieve the isolated facts and when they happened, but mostly I remember that terrifying repetition, the faces of rejection, even from friends, the questions without answers, the loss of confidence people showed in my son, more than in the police. And always, in those moments of recounting Jorge's story, the nightmare that I hardly dared imagine: the eventual reality of Jorge, his life in a secret cell. That son of mine made into a piece of meat.

The day after Jorge's disappearance, Raúl, excited and apprehensive, came over to the family's house. He was obviously in a state of tremendous anxiety.

"Calm down, Raúl!" I shout. I don't understand anything that's going on, but I react immediately. It's clear that there's been some mistake here. "Why five cars if Jorge didn't do anything? All he was doing was trying to get some prisoners released—that's all. We've got to find him and straighten out the mistake. Then they'll let him go."

"But you don't understand, Mama. They took him away!" Raúl screams again.

Toto wakes up. Everything is much too confused. Raúl starts stuffing some clothes into his backpack and says he's going to a friend's house for a few days. Just in case they come looking for him here.

"Why do you need to hide if you haven't done anything, for God's sake?" I shout at him.

Toto gets dressed and says he has to go out and look for Jorge and that there isn't any time to lose. "We've got to find him and get things cleared up, that's all. Then they'll let him go. What are you waiting for? Get dressed!" Humberto shouts at me and at that moment we both remember Alejandra.

"Alie, do you want to go to your grandparents or come with us?" we ask her. She answers by putting her eleven year old self into our ancient Chevrolet.

The car bolts off. It's almost ten in the morning. It's only a few blocks to the 8th Precinct station. Toto tells me to calm down because the way I'm acting I'll just make things worse.

When we get to the police station Toto explains to the official that the plainclothes policeman came to Jorge's house and took him away.

"Well, how do you know they were police?"

"Because of the weapons they were carrying. And people in our neighborhood said they were the police . . . ."

"Do you want to make a formal complaint? Do you even know if the boy was taken prisoner?"

Toto repeats himself. "We want to clear things up because it's evident that there's been a mistake here. Look . . . ."

The official is as nice and well behaved as a princess, but after delaying us for more than an hour with question after question, he remembers that we should be talking to someone at the 5th Precinct station. Frightened, and reeling from this first failure, and feeling slightly ridiculous, we go to the 5th Precinct. Alejandra tags along behind with her doll. The new police chief is a fat man with red hands. He says he regrets that they have given us the wrong information. "If you live in the 8<sup>th</sup> Precinct, in City Bell, even though your son was taken from another place, the complaint has to be made in City Bell. As much as we might want to, we can't do anything for you here. Please, Senora, calm yourself."

We return to the 8th Precinct station. They tell us again that we should go to the 5<sup>th</sup> precinct station. Everything is totally and infernally confused. We're just a toy to them.

Toto and I still don't think they're lying. "Why would they lie to you, Hebe? They're just imbeciles who don't really know the regulations. That's all. Don't worry. We'll go see a lawyer—you remember—Maria Elena's brother. She's sure he'll know what to do."

Raúl had told us over and over, "That paper, the one they call a habeas corpus, is the first thing to do, Mama. The problem is, who knows how to do it. We need someone to help us with it."

The lawyer, Maria Elena's brother, is waiting for us at his house. He's been informed about Jorge and he's afraid. He's in a state of panic just thinking about what could happen to the rest of his family. He's smart and he knows all about the habeas corpus, but he doesn't want to do it. "I apologize," he keeps saying "but I can't. I'm afraid. Everything is madness now."

"Okay then, damn it, at least you can explain to me how it's done and I'll write it myself." I'd never seen Humberto so upset. He listens to the lawyer's hurried instructions. It's obvious that Maria Elena's brother is unwilling to spend even a minute more with us.

We bang the door closed. What's going on? The world has gone crazy and we're living in some kind of hell.

"Why are we doing a habeas corpus if tomorrow Jorge will be back? By then all the mix-up will be straightened out and Jorge will come back, Toto, I'm sure of it."

"We have to do it because Raúl said to."

There are still a few people who might help us. We remember a distant relative, a policeman who lives in Castelar. Between the heat and the long drive to see him, we feel more confused than ever. When we finally get to Castelar our relative seems pleasant enough. He inquires for the family. Alejandra listens. She looks at the policeman with her big, dark eyes and asks about her brother as if she were an adult.

"All right," says the policeman at last. "It's clear that this has to do with the Army, or the Federal Police or the combined forces. You can dismiss any idea of a kidnapping. This is something official, but we won't be able to find out anything about it."

Before we leave he reminds us that the habeas corpus won't help us much. "It's a formality that's just good for helping relatives to calm down, but it isn't worth a blessed thing."

We're bewildered and a sense of helpless desperation is already insinuating itself into our lives. We know we shouldn't let ourselves get disheartened. We shouldn't be thinking about Jorge now, imagining him in some jail. We should be concentrating on what we're going to do next.

Now it's drizzling and the road is slippery. In the back seat Alejandra has finally caved in and is crying in silence. I know that I should try to console her, to explain to her the inexplicable.

Then, against my will, I have my first images of Jorge. I think about poor Maria Elena who is expecting a baby. It had never occurred to her that anything worse than losing the child could happen to her. But what was I doing, talking about losses? If everything could just be cleared up, tomorrow we would have Jorge home again!

I keep wondering about who we can count on—who there is who can help us. "We have to do the habeas corpus," Toto keeps repeating. "We have to do that blessed paper. Raúl said so!"

I tell him, no, that it's going to take more time to write the paper and get it through the infernal Argentine bureaucracy than it is to find our son and get him back home. "It's all a question of clearing things up, Toto."

Then suddenly I picture Jorge being thrown into the car. "All right," I say and I grab the habeas corpus form. I reverse myself and say that, yes; we certainly do have to do the paper. In the glove compartment I find a small pencil with a blunt point. Toto begins to realize the horror of all this, as if he were just waking up from a nightmare. Who knows where Jorge could be . . . ?

"Okay, let's get started." I shout. "You dictate." And I start writing.

> "Señor Humberto Bonafini, living on Calle 531, #1450 in Tolosa, document no. 5.108,258. He presents a writ of habeas corpus on behalf of his son, Jorge Omar Bonafini, 26 years old, teacher at the School of Exact Sciences, who disappeared from his home on Tuesday, the eighth day of this month . . . ."

Then Toto puts a sudden end to our effort. He refuses to drive any more at this hour on a rainy night when everything is all so confused. "I can't go on. I just can't go on." We decide to spend the night in Luján. We put all our pesos together and settle into a cheap hotel . . . We sleep with our clothes on, but it is a brief, deep sleep—as if we had been hit over the head.

The next morning we are back on the road. We drive in silence, each of us thinking about what more can be done, and about who can help. There has to be someone. Our confusion forces us to ask for help from people we don't even know. We knock on their doors and try to explain what happened to Jorge. All we get are a series of incredulous reactions. We feel like mindless robots impelled by some strange energy that brings us to innumerable jails, sacristies and judges' offices. The answer is always "No".

I also think about my brother in the hospital—maybe he's dying right now. We have to keep caring about other people, but we have to go on looking for Jorge. All this makes us even more desperate. It seems to paralyze us. After about a century of driving we finally arrive in La Plata and go straight to the hospital. My brother is more emaciated than ever. He has that dark color of cancer and he smells of drugs.

We go on telling him lies: that Jorge is finishing his dissertation on the laser, that he has to hand it in in a couple of weeks, but that when it's all done he'll come see him and that, for now, he sends his love.


Our house in City Bell is deserted. Maybe the telephone will ring and someone will give us good news! Hope fades. The telephone is mute and the hours pass.

"We have to go to El Dique to talk with our parents, Hebe. Someone has to tell them."

Once again the three of us get in the Chevrolet, chasing after another nightmare. Because to tell my parents was a way of admitting, horribly, that there would be no immediate solution, that we couldn't go on disguising the absence of their grandson who had always visited them so often.

Our tactics to soften the blow fail miserably when we're face to face with this old married couple who seem so serene. Despite all my efforts to make light of it, the truth comes rushing out with no masquerading.

Papa prefers to deny everything, to think that the whole thing is a cruel joke. Mama screams. When she finally quiets down, she says, "We were having such luck! What did my grandson do?"

"He didn't do anything, Mama. He was working so that other people, just like him, might get out of the same place where he is now. I swear to you, Mama, there's no mystery to it."

Nine days after Jorge's arrest (or should I just call it "kidnapping"?), my brother loses consciousness and is talking nonsense. Finally he dies. Raúl can't bear his seclusion and comes out of hiding to be at the wake. I tell him that he shouldn't worry about us, but he insists. "Mama, I need you too."

After the burial Raúl comes back to the house with his backpack full of dirty clothes. I feel sick to my stomach, but I wash all of Raúl's clothes and I make dinner. The four of us eat, in silence, but together, and feeling safer. Despite our fear and our exhaustion, we all feel stronger with Raúl in the house. Even though we might not want to, we have to go on living.

## Habeas Corpus

"Wake up, Toto—please!" In a few minutes the alarm would go off and Humberto was still clinging to those last few minutes of rest. I didn't want to waste any time

"In the middle of the night I thought of someone. Russo, you remember Russo, the judge, the father of the girl who was a friend of Jorge's. We saw her a couple of times at school. I'm sure he could help us." A little later I talked it over with Raúl and it seemed a good idea to him, too,

At nine in the morning I boarded the micro bus that would take me to Russo's office. His secretary made me wait a good while before she opened the heavy wooden doors for me.

"Russo. How are you?" I said. "You remember me. I'm Hebe Bonafini. Your daughter and my son were good friends at school."

"I'm having trouble placing you . . . . It's so long ago. Your son is Daniel?"

"No, no, Judge. It's Jorge, Jorge Bonafini—he used to study a lot at your house. Later he went into physics."

"Vaguely, vaguely . . . .". The judge said that he didn't remember my son (even though Jorge had been a close friend of his daughter and the judge used to keep an obsessive watch over her). In any case, he must have heard from his daughter what was happening at the university. But no matter—I felt forced to give the details of Jorge's abduction once again. As I did, he injected comments like "what barbarity!". He finished things off by saying, in a voice somewhere between incredulous and distressed, "Are you very sure of your facts?"

"Señor, I only want to know if you're going to help us."

He answered that to help us would be to enter into the wolf's mouth and that really, apart from the habeas corpus, there was nothing that could be done. "You came here to ask me something that puts me at risk and isn't going to save your son."

I pressed him for a decision "because if you don't help me, you'll make me think that the judges in my country are just ornaments." I felt that I had to shock him in some way, to break that deceitful amiability he was using to make me realize that he wouldn't lift a finger for me.

"Let's be honest, Señor. Tell me directly if you're not going to help me. Don't just give me the run-around."

He smiled a little, the way doctors smile when they're with someone seriously ill. "Calm down," he said. And I answered, "Señor Judge, I'm not excited. I'm indignant!"

At that point he chose to get rid of me. He repeated that, as a favor, he would draw up the habeas corpus and that he would think about taking some kind of action. "I don't promise it, you understand. It's putting my whole family in jeopardy because of a third party." Then he opened those great wooden doors and showed me out.

## Palermo

In March, after a month of frustration, Maria Elena called me, shouting her message into the telephone. "A girl at the university said Jorge must be in Palermo in Buenos Aires. She says there's an army installation there where they hold all the prisoners from La Plata."

Could this be true?

Toto had had to go back to his job at the refinery. Raúl was working too; we needed his salary. I kept the family going, but I was the least productive in terms of money. There seemed only one solution: I would have to solve everything by myself—alone. I was going to have to take the train, all by myself, and get off in an unknown city. "And who knows where in the world Palermo is? Well, somehow, I'll manage. If I leave good and early . . . ."

As I got ready to leave the next morning Raúl queried me. "What are you doing?" he asked as he watched me lay out some of Jorge's clothes.

"I'm just putting together a little bundle with some clean clothes for Jorge. If I explain it all to the police, I'm sure they'll get them to him."

I took the train at seven in the morning. It was full of sleepy people, men in suits looking out the windows without seeing anything. A few women were carrying plastic bags. Among their faces I recognized one I'd seen before. She was a little older than me, with gray hair and dark circles under her eyes. She looked away when I glanced at her. But now I remembered—we'd seen each other a few times at the 5th Precinct station in La Plata.

Finally, after asking for a lot of directions along the way, I arrived in Palermo around nine thirty. "First Army Corps" it said on the gray cement arches over the well-guarded bars at the entrance. The gate was opened for me and an armed soldier stuck right with me until I got inside. I showed my documents and then they asked me to wait. I was thinking that Jorge would be there, in that building with the rectangular windows. Then another soldier took me to another room.

"I want to speak to the person in charge here," I say. "Of course, Señora, but you're going to have to wait a little." I answer that I'll do whatever is necessary. But each new step takes an hour. After a while, a meticulous policeman has me walk through a passageway with bars on either side and then into a bare office with no place to sit down. I have to wait by standing for another hour before I'm taken to a room with two long wooden benches.

I'm not alone there. A tall, bald man, in a well-cut suit, is hiding his face in his hands. He is sitting there, almost immobile. He doesn't talk. From time to time he looks at his watch. He gives the impression of having spent hours in that same position.

A woman is also waiting. She has some papers in her hands and she is standing up, leaning against the wall. She is better dressed that I am and her hair is nicely fixed. I am the only one carrying a little tied-up bundle.

I look at the floor and I begin to count the tiles. There are 64. How much longer will they make me wait?

A soldier comes to inform us that in a few minutes they will have us go into the office. I wonder who the others are and what their problems are.

According to the man's watch, it's after two o'clock. I can't bear to count the tiles again. I get up and walk over to the door with the bars. Down the hall two officials carrying large weapons are smoking. And they are laughing. One of them takes a wad of tobacco out of his mouth and looks at me.

I respond by shouting at them. "How long are you going to keep us here? How long are you going to make us wait? I've been here for five hours, without a bathroom, without even a glass of water and you just keep saying that we have to wait. Don't any of you have mothers?"

The officials look at me and smile and then they walk away. I shout again, and I make it even louder so those miserable men who were laughing will hear me. I start screaming, with my eyes closed, grabbing onto the bars. Each scream was giving me back the strength I'd lost by waiting, was giving me a reason and a right to be there.

Someone took me by the shoulders and walked me away from the door. "Not like that. All you'll do is get taken away too."

The man said he was called Emilio. He didn't take my hand and he hardly smiled as he said: "The first thing is to have patience. I myself began searching for my daughter nine months ago." [EN-H: Mignone]

It's not possible . . . nine months. Just the thought that something like that could happen with Jorge would drive me crazy. At the same time I had never even considered that possibility. My having brought clothes for Jorge now seemed ridiculous, a sign of my stupid naiveté. It wasn't possible—nine months . . . .

The woman was talking with an official who had come to tell us that they wouldn't be able to see us at all that day. It was more than three in the afternoon. The woman took me by the arm. "Call me Ida". She told me that she was looking for her husband. I said good-bye to Emilio and wished him luck in finding his daughter. "You and I will meet again," he responded sadly, almost with resignation.

Later Ida walked with me for a couple of blocks to the bus stop. "They beat up my husband something fierce," she said. I didn't want to hear any more, but the phrase kept hammering in my head all the way back to La Plata. Why a beating if an interrogation would clear up any doubts?

## Conflicts

When I got back home Alejandra was looking out the window, waiting for me. She had an enormous smile on her face but it fell to pieces when she saw that I was still carrying the little bundle. I didn't come back with Jorge, and neither had I managed to get his clothes to him, wherever he might be.

My young daughter's face made me return to reality—not that the search wasn't real. It was. In fact it was the most concrete thing that I was able to do. But what I mean is that my daughter was letting me know that life should go on, even though Jorge wasn't with us. That contradiction made me feel sad: nothing had stopped here at home. The days were passing, my eleven-year-old daughter needed her mother, she would be hungry. I would have to fix dinner, to ask her about school, to look at her notebooks. I gave her a big hug and thought, "Alejandrita, a month of your childhood has already been an inferno—you should be playing with your friends." She just looked at me without understanding too much. All she wanted to know was why they had taken her brother away.

Should I talk with Toto and Raúl in secret about Jorge and try to keep her from knowing that a diabolical bureaucracy was coming between her brother and us? No, I thought, if the world, if the country was, indeed, a criminal bureaucracy, I wasn't going to give her a fictitious picture of it. I wasn't going to bring her up so totally protected that, sooner or later, she would be shocked by disillusionment.

I heated up the dinner that I had left ready in the morning. Toto set the table in silence.

"Nine months, do you understand? Why do they hold them so long without freeing them? Do they make them work?" I couldn't bear the thought of nine months without Jorge.

## Memories

At night, as much as I might have wanted to resist it, my memory betrayed me and all kinds of things from the past came back to me as I lay in bed with Toto beside me. (Was he really sleeping or was he just pretending, the way I often did?). I kept very quiet, with my eyes open, in the darkness and silence of that room. That way I would be able to remember everything perfectly without any distortion.

As I was recollecting our past, Jorge was with me. Now I was remembering his and Maria Elena's wedding day. They had wanted a ceremony in their own home. It was the most important day of their lives and they were joyously exuberant. Maria Elena was lovely in her white pant suit with its yellow bow and a matching yellow chignon. And Jorge had finally been convinced that he should wear the only acceptable jacket in Humberto's closet. Their small living room was beautiful with flowers, roses and white carnations, the embroidered tablecloth, food, cider, wine and champagne.

Besides their love, they had other things to share. They were a couple with their feet on the ground—not just two people in love in a static relationship. They worked together, protested together and shared ideals.

Before the priest began the service, Jorge passed out the words to a song he had written for Maria Elena to celebrate the life that they were beginning. With guitars playing in the background, we all began to sing as Jorge and Maria Elena put on their rings. It was a beautiful song, imagining a simple, radiant future with promises of love, of children who would come into a different world because together Jorge and Maria Elena were going to change that world. It was the song of a man in love, but also the song of a happy, militant, almost euphoric, commitment to life and to the future.

## *Blows*

At the end of March, exactly one year after the coup, we received an official communication that made us despair all the more.

March 24, 1977

Humberto Bonafini

I hereby inform you that because of the terms of Book I of the Code of Criminal Procedures in case No. 26,271 which includes the petition for the writ of Habeas Corpus on behalf of Jorge Omar Bonafini, the following resolution has been handed down: La Plata, March 24, 1977. Considering proceedings and pronouncements, I deny the petition for Habeas Corpus on behalf of Jorge Omar Bonafini.

Written, notified, and filed.

Leopoldo Russo, Federal Judge of La Plata.

The rejection of the writ of habeas corpus for Jorge was a decided, but not surprising, disappointment for Hebe and Toto. Of the hundreds of such writs filed on behalf of disappeared people, they knew of none that had ever been granted.

But neither of them was prepared for another event, also timed to mark the anniversary of the coup: the gunning down of the journalist Rodolfo Walsh on March 25th, 1977.

During the year after the coup, Walsh wrote a series of open letters highly critical of Argentina's military government and delivered them to his friends and colleagues. On March 24, 1977, he again wrote an open letter to the junta. He stated that the letter had been provoked by the censoring of the press, the persecution of intellectuals, the raid on his house, the assassinations of close friends and the loss of a daughter who was killed combating the forces of this "accursed government"—a government, he said, that had implemented the most intense state of terror that Argentine society had ever experienced. Walsh specifically accused the junta of having turned Argentina's major military installations into concentration camps where no judges, lawyers, journalists, or international observers were allowed to enter. He further stated that 6000 writs of habeas corpus had been turned down in the past year. He cited the junta for refusing to publish the names of prisoners, for their secret and systematic execution of prisoners, for carrying out genocide, and for hurling prisoners, sometimes drugged, but still alive, into the sea from Fokker planes of the 1st Aerial Brigade.

Walsh concluded his open letter by accusing the junta of supporting an economy that was guided by the International Monetary Fund, an economy that only helped the old land-owning oligarchy, the new class of speculators and a small group of international monopolies (ITT, U.S. Steel, Esso, Siemens and automobile manufacturers). Instead of alleviating the lives of the working classes who for years had been crying out for reform, he claimed that the junta was making life much worse for the impoverished multitudes. [RJW: 415-424]

Walsh knew that he would be persecuted for his letter, but he declared that he was determined to be faithful to the promise he had committed himself to many years earlier of giving testimony in difficult moments.

The day after he circulated this letter to the junta Walsh was ambushed in Buenos Aires and shot dead.

# Chapter 4

## Hebe and the Plaza de Mayo

*Hebe Reacts*

When Jorge first disappeared there was a tremendous void, a feeling of desperation, a bewildering shock. I remembered a mother of a disappeared child who had told me that she had spent seven months waiting in a rocking chair, rocking back and forth like some old grandmother, paralyzed. For myself, I needed to react with an almost frenetic activity, to recuperate from the loss by doing things. The search was transformed into a dizziness that kept me from thinking, but that ignited my inner strength and propelled me into the streets, to the ministries, to write letters. To work was the only way not to feel that I was dead, humiliated and empty.

There wasn't time to wonder how our children were doing or how they were bearing up under the blows. We didn't think; we acted. And behind the action was always hope. Not to take action was to surrender the children. To abandon them.

I never sat down and cried, I never screamed or shut myself in for days to sniff the clothes that my child had left behind. The same thing was true for other mothers. We didn't say "They beat them, they torture them, they drag them off, they knock them unconscious." We would say "We have to send a letter to Pio Laghi, the Papal Nuncio. We must see Cardinal Primatesta". We had to work until we dropped, until we were completely spent. That way we could sleep at night.

## Buenos Aires

I began to notice that the faces were repeating themselves in the courts and police stations of La Plata. But I didn't speak with the other women though it was obvious that the same thing that had happened to me had happened to them. Finally I realized the time had come when I had exhausted all the possibilities of searching in La Plata; I would have to go to Buenos Aires. But I was apprehensive.

I arrive in Buenos Aires and go into the coffee shop at the Constitution Bus Station. Maria Elena and Raúl are coming to the city too and we've decided to meet here. I know they might be late and that I'd better make myself comfortable. I look around at all the people just passing through. The young people I'm waiting for are not among them. I reach in my purse for some paper and I find a small pad. Almost without thinking I begin to write.

> I am sitting by a window. I see many kinds of people passing by. Each of them obviously has his problems. They are sad, pensive, lifeless. They're alone, yet a part of the multitude. I am also alone. I am waiting, and while I wait, I drink coffee.
>
> I am thinking, thinking. Where are you, Jorge my son? You are in some place, perhaps nearer than I realize. I am with you; I imagine you thin, bent over, somewhere, but no longer with us. Every day, and even more at night, I see you coming home, and I listen for your knocks

*at the door. I open it and there is only silence, pure silence,*
*hanging over everything.*

*Outside the bus station, there's a changing scene,*
*the incessant passing of people. From the window I always*
*see young couples. I envy them and I think about you.*
*Your image stands out among all the others, brilliant,*
*luminous. What are you thinking about, my beloved,*
*you who were always doing so much thinking? What*
*now occupies your thoughts? How hard everything is,*
*Jorge. No matter how much you imagine it, it's never the*
*same in reality. I know that your great intelligence will*
*help you get through this critical time more easily. Close*
*your eyes, as I do now, and think of me. I'm sure that, if*
*you do, everything is going to pass very quickly.*

In Buenos Aires I saw those same faces in the courts, in the office of the Minister of the Interior. As we all stood there in the same lines we only gave each other shy sidelong glances. In the beginning I only made a disguised effort to fish for a little information. But there was really no need to ask questions because each of us repeated our own story dozens of times to the changing faces at the little windows.

It was early in April when I began to talk with some of the other women. Our conversations were limited to the habeas corpus petitions and the best way of writing them and of identifying the judges that weren't granting them. I didn't give any of the women my name or my telephone number. We were anonymous, distrustful people, united by our paperwork and the lives we were trying to recover. Mothers without children, wives without husbands or brothers. Women looking for other people—a precarious company caught up in the solitary business of dealing with a bureaucracy.

One day the bus went by the side door of the Casa Rosada in the Plaza de Mayo. I was determined not to think about Videla, or the junta, or the Doctrine of National

Security. I only wanted to keep alive the hope I got from that little window where a nice police woman, almost syrupy, would wait on me with the promise of interceding and would preoccupy herself personally with my problems. "Leave me your telephone number and your address and I'll let you know. I'll try to do everything possible; I promise you. Poor soul! Your case is so moving . . . ."

And all of us left our addresses and we secretly clung to that promise, believing it was true. Of course, nobody cared about us personally. It was just a trap where they got a lot of information to put into their evil filing system that had our information and home addresses—our X-rays.

That afternoon my steps and my itinerary coincided with the ones of that gray-haired woman with the pronounced dark circles under her eyes, whom I had seen days earlier when I had gone to Palermo on the train and visited the First Army Corps. Both of us took the subway and rode together to the Plaza de Mayo, to the office of the Minister of the Interior. Then, about two weeks later, we saw each other again and the woman said, "We could go back to La Plata together on the bus, if that seems like a good idea to you." I agreed and we sat together in the back of the bus. But we sat in silence. Then I began to ask myself why I had accepted her invitation if I intended to remain mute. In reality, I was wondering if she had a child who had disappeared. Perhaps her child might be sharing the cell and some meals with my son just as we were sharing the seat, silently, not knowing how to get to know each other under such circumstances.

It was she who spoke first. She didn't give her name, but she said she was looking for her twenty-four-year-old daughter. They had taken her away five months ago. Her daughter was pregnant. I was shocked. How could that woman go on living if her daughter was a prisoner and soon to give birth? I refused to believe that things were really so grave, so rough. I didn't know the woman's name but I began to feel a tremendous sense of solidarity with her pain. I was beginning to think that my case was not so serious.

As the bus sped along, I began to feel a bond with that woman. And somehow, I felt understood. She went on talking about her daughter and about the paperwork that brought no results. Although she sounded sad, she seemed a little released from her own suffering, as if she had gone beyond the moments of confusion that I myself was now experiencing. "We are many more than you believe", she finally said "and we are beginning to work."

"To work?" I asked. I had no idea what that word could mean in this situation. The woman responded that a group of mothers were doing their paperwork together and were arranging for interviews with influential people who could help them.

I asked her if it might help if I joined the group. "I feel so alone. Every day it gets harder and harder to keep on with all this paperwork. I'm beginning to have the feeling that they're pulling the wool over my eyes, that, really, it's all for nothing."

The woman smiled. She understood. Our initial distance had evaporated. She said that on the coming Thursday a group of mothers would be getting together in the afternoon in the Plaza de Mayo. [EN-I: Plaza de Mayo] They were going to sign a petition or perhaps they would have an interview with a priest. It might be a good idea to come, "the more mothers, the better". I said that I'd think it over. (Something in me was still asking if we weren't creating too much of a commotion for a bit of nonsense. I really thought, or at least I hoped, that all this sad confusion would surely be resolved soon.) The woman stood up and shook hands with me and began to walk down the aisle of the bus.

"Don't forget. Thursday at two. On the dot."

Back home in City Bell I was still struggling with the problem of joining the women in the Plaza.

"Do you think I should go?"

"Of course!" Raúl shouted. "The only chance we have is if we all join together and show our strength. And let those vicious people in the junta know that they can't get the best of us."

"Just a moment." Toto cautioned.

He always stopped to consider everything, to calculate the risks, as if he were bringing his first impulses under control. And I'm grateful for it.

"I'm afraid", he said. "Let's just think which would be worse. Suppose they should break into our house? What if they take Raúl away?—or Maria Elena? And how would you feel if they tried to give us a scare by threatening Alejandra?"

## The Plaza de Mayo

I walk around the Plaza de Mayo. It isn't quite two. I haven't seen the woman from the train with the dark circles under her eyes. I'm feeling nervous; I want to be sure that she'll be in the Plaza when I get there. Suddenly I ask myself why I'm afraid. What was wrong, when you came right down to it, with my joining those women? Didn't I remember the billboards on Bolivar Street that proclaimed the official slogan, "The country progresses", in blue letters on a white background, just like our national flag?

A few women are already there in the plaza, near the pyramid, standing together beside a bench. Not more than 10. The woman from the train still hasn't come, but walking toward me is another woman, short, with brown hair and attractive features. She has solid arms and workers' hands.

Her body makes me think of a great fortress. The weather is cool for April, but she is wearing a loose cotton T-shirt. I try to explain who I am and how I happen to be there: "a lady from La Plata told me on the bus". It is all very vague, but the woman begins to smile. "Ah! Yes", she says finally. "She spoke of you. She said you'd be here. Come on."

The women all appeared extremely hurried. They were talking quickly, softly, their voices bumping into one another. They were circulating a paper. "By chance we got hold of a typewriter," the woman whispered to me. "We wrote a letter to President Videla and we pleaded for our children. Now we're signing it before we deliver it to the Secretary. Sign if you want".

She—"call me Azucena"—was conversing with the others, while a second woman took two pens out of her bag and a third woman came up to me: "You've gone to the League, haven't you? The League for Human Rights. No? Ah! And I suppose you didn't go to the Permanent Assembly, or Emilio's group either."

"Wait," I said. "I think I know him. He was the man I saw in Palermo." Then she told me that Emilio Mignone, that bald, patient man, was trying to organize the fathers and that he was a lawyer. But she and the other women wanted to do this on their own. "As mothers, it seems to me that we feel differently and that other groups don't understand us. We think that it's better to negotiate alone, by ourselves. I don't know."

Then another woman told me that she and Azucena had gone various times to speak with Father Emilio Grasselli, a powerful man who was secretary to the Military Chaplain. "Several of us went. Azucena, Maria Adela, Dora, Juanita. But the receptionist wouldn't let us in. You go, and you make an appointment for the next week, but you don't find out anything. At times it seems like we're just getting the run-around."

The women continued to pass around the paper and to explain what it was about to a couple of women who had just arrived. The city kept up its rhythm at our backs; people didn't even seem to realize we were there. Men were hurrying by because the banks were closing; some retired men, completely indifferent to us, were taking the sun. We women may have looked like alumnae of some school that was planning a reunion. Most of us would be about my age or somewhere in their 50s. Azucena moved quickly, like a young woman, but she was somewhat older. She and I became friends.

I agreed with the petition and I signed. I did it with a large, clear signature so that the President would read my name and it would be engraved on his eyes. Also, so that he would know that my son's name gave me no shame.

We left the Plaza saying that we would see each other there again the following Thursday. At that time none of us thought that our waiting for our children would be longer than a couple of months, nor that our early attempts to find our children would some day become this painful story. Not one of those women took any notes about the small things we were doing. Who could have known then all that would happen?

## A Decisive Turn

I didn't know then that at that precise moment my life was getting ready for a decisive turn. During those months of searching for Jorge, I thought that all my activity was just temporary. Now, little by little, it was being converted into the thing that the gray-haired woman on the bus to La Plata had talked about—a real job.

For the time being I was trying to do two jobs at the same time as best I could. Life, in the meantime, had become an inferno. Our pleasant routine in City Bell, that made no allowances for the unforeseen, had been buried under all the hurrying around, the bad news, and the trips to Buenos Aires. I had to use the money that Toto and I had put aside for our vacation for the continual drain of bus fare to the city.

There was so much to do, and it all took so long, that I wasn't able to keep things organized at home, to guarantee that life would go on as it always had for the past twenty-five years. Things were going at a feverish pace—though I admit this had its advantages. It didn't leave any time to go crazy with desperation.

It was obvious that each of us mothers would have to make adjustments—and each of our families would have to adjust too. With all his work at the refinery, Humberto didn't have any time left over for filing bureaucratic papers. However, there were new things that he would have to learn if we wanted to assure the stability of our family: to do a little housework and to act as a mother to Alejandra while I was away from home.

Meanwhile, my demands on myself were multiplying and I couldn't let myself be inattentive to them. I was divided in a hundred directions. I would get home about midnight and get up at six in the morning to leave the breakfast ready for the others. But I still felt I had to keep alive that woman I had always been, no matter the cost, pushing myself to my limits—and past my tiredness. I didn't want this woman who cooked dinner and sewed dusters with her mother to be relegated to second place.

For someone who only knew the world that the radio and television let her glimpse, the shock of reality was traumatic and I was filled with all kinds of fears. Although Humberto understood what I was doing and encouraged me, how long would he put up with my being away so much? Would we be able to adapt to the new situation? I was afraid too because I had the sense that, with all the

changes in our routine, things were out of control. I was forced to see Raúl less and Alejandra accused me of being more of a mother for the son who wasn't there than for the children who were still at home. I felt all churned up, frightened and a little guilty. My head was going round and round from so much sadness and pain—and so many endless things I should be doing.

# CHAPTER 5

## THE MOTHERS' EARLY ACTIONS

### First Times in the Plaza

The first time the Mothers went to the Plaza was April 30, 1977 and there was just a handful of women. The Mothers group was created because in the other organizations of the relatives of the disappeared there wasn't any sense of closeness. There was always some intervening desk, something bureaucratic about those groups. But in the Plaza we all felt equal. We all had children who had disappeared and we were all looking in the same places for them. The Plaza really brought us together in such a way that we didn't feel any distance between us. That sense of equality was very important to us.

We wanted other mothers to know about us so we decided we should go around to the Police Department, the Minister of the Interior, and even house to house— looking for more mothers to join us in the Plaza. If we saw some woman sitting off alone and crying we would try to get her to come to the Plaza. Going from house to house was hard because it meant you might be followed or that people would call the police to ask who this woman was who was asking if there was a disappeared person in that family. Or sometimes people simply refused to open their doors to us. But if we went to five houses we could usually count on two of them getting our message.

## Defying the Police

As the weeks went by, our numbers grew and we became better organized. Each time we came together we felt stronger, safer, less afraid. By the end of September 1977 we were more than fifty women. But it was sad—each new mother meant another disappeared person.

Now as we walked around in the Plaza every Thursday afternoon, we had moments of feeling defiant, almost invincible. We could see the balcony of the Casa Rosada. We were beginning to disturb President Videla. Fifty old women marching around together can't be an alumnae group from some school.

We were always expecting that someone would question us. But the truth is that the police didn't know what to do with us. If there was any goodness left in their hearts, it was the verse of some masochistic tango about "the poor old woman". They thought that we were crazed by grief, that we would stay only until we got tired of standing there with so many varicose veins or until a heart attack struck one of us.

By the time our group in the Plaza had grown to sixty or seventy, the policeman in the Plaza began to threaten us for just sitting on the benches there. "All right, you can't do this here. There's a state of siege and this is a meeting. Keep moving. Keep walking." And he struck out at us with his nightstick. It was the policeman who made us march; we hadn't even thought of marching.

When we began coming to the Plaza every Thursday we would walk around, arm in arm. Gradually we became more confident; our consciences were firmer. We insisted on walking around the pyramid. After a while a policeman asked one of the mothers for her documents and, quite innocently, she gave them to him. The next time we were there, the same thing happened. The third time they asked for one of the mother's documents, we decided that every last one of us would give them our documents. By then there were almost three hundred of us so it took them a long, long time to identify us and then return the papers to each one of us. Really it was an important action for us to take. First, it was an act of unity (all or nothing) and it was also our way of putting an end to the game of asking us for our documents.

A little later the police were dispatched once again. "This is a demonstration and there is marshal law. Keep moving, ladies, keep moving." We began to walk two together, arm in arm. We knew that the most important thing was to keep closing the circle, but imperceptibly, each time closer to the pyramid. But the police brought reinforcements. They blocked us from getting close to it. But we went on walking and conversing, looking at the back of the head of the mothers in front of us. I could see the back of the French nun, Alice Domon, who walked arm in arm with Mary Ponce. Further ahead I saw the strong figure of Azucena with her sturdy arms, dressed in a light pullover in this springtime coolness. We kept on marching.

## Dead End in a Church

Sometimes the Mothers met in churches. One time, soon after I first joined them, we were in a church that was more or less full because it was a saint's day. Some of the mothers said that we should always meet in churches because it was more protected and more "spiritual", less wrenching, and that being in a church made us feel closer to our children. As if the church might make us feel less afraid.

Then a little before the mass began, Azucena went up to the side of the altar that had still not been lit. She left a sheet of paper there on which she had written, "Father, we are mothers whose children have been illegally detained. We don't know where the authorities are holding our children and we aren't allowed to see them. But people don't believe us. They give us strange looks. We even have relatives who have stopped coming to see us. We need to have you briefly mention our children in your sermon. We ask you in the name of the love of God and the Christian faith."

Azucena left the note and returned to her seat. Nobody seemed to have noticed us. A few minutes later, the altar boy and the curate were preparing the altar and opened the New Testament. It was then that the curate saw the note. He picked it up and gave it to the priest who was standing off to one side, adjusting his vestment. We saw the priest read it and put it in a pocket of his cassock.

We said "Good. Now we're all set. Now we only have to wait for the sermon." But as soon as the service began we saw that things weren't going well—the priest didn't even look at us. It was as if he were giving the mass for everyone but us.

The time for the sermon arrived and how sad it was when he dedicated exactly twenty minutes to the problem of Christian faith and divine patience.

## Foreign Visitors

When important people from foreign countries came to Buenos Aires, the Mothers showed up when nobody else was in the streets. When Terence Todman, United States Assistant Secretary of State for Latin American Affairs, came, about thirty of us Mothers went to Plaza San Martín and we announced to everyone there that we had children who had disappeared. Videla sent a message ordering us to leave the plaza. We decided not to leave. So we linked arms and stayed there. Then, to hold our ground, we all hung on to a column. So they sent in soldiers with helmets, armed as if for war, to force us to leave. And we told them that, no, we really weren't going to leave.

Then they took up their weapons and aimed at us and as they yelled, "Ready, Aim", we all shouted, *"Fire!"* Our shouting made the journalists who were there to see Terence Todman come over to find out who those women were who had taken such a strong stand. It made the news in several newspapers.

In November of 1977, Cyrus Vance, the United States Secretary of State, came to Argentina. (He later wrote a State Department report accusing Argentina of gross human rights violations.) When he went to the Plaza San Martín to put flowers on the monument of the revered leader José San Martín, we shouted out once again about our disappeared children. And once again we caught the attention of the press, and there is a photo taken of us at that time that was shown around the world. People from all over saw this picture, but in our country it was never shown. There was absolutely nothing about it in the local papers and very few people in Argentina even heard about our demonstration that day.

## March to Luján

In early October of 1977, the Catholic community of Buenos Aires had begun planning a march of thousands of young people to Luján. A small group of mothers had tea at Las Violetas, a cafe, to discuss the march. Azucena said that it would be a good idea if we all joined the annual pilgrimage to Luján because that's how we would make ourselves known. We agreed because, in addition to that reason, we had many Catholic mothers who wanted to go to pray the rosary. But the mothers would be coming from different places and we had to agree on where we'd meet, and how we'd recognize one another.

"I know what we could do," Eva, one of the mothers, says. "We could wear something that will distinguish us from far away, so we can find one another. A kerchief on our heads, for example."

"Or a mantilla. But we don't all have mantillas. Better a kerchief."

"Yes," says another woman. "Or better still a baby diaper; it looks like a kerchief but it will make us feel better, closer to our children. A baby's diaper on the head—good. We've all kept some; we'll iron one carefully before the procession. Now we have to spread the word in La Plata and everywhere we can, so there'll be plenty of us. We have to drag out the mothers who are just sitting at home in their armchairs. We have to convince them to come with us.

The day of the march the diapers leap out at the sun in the sea of people walking around. We begin to come together, first two, then three. Further on we encounter another small group. The diapers multiply and stun the rest of the pilgrims who don't take them as any coincidence. When we get to the plaza in front of the basilica in Lujan we're a good-sized group. Fifteen or twenty of us come together and, standing in a circle, we say the rosary for the children who are no longer with us, for the children who have disappeared.

Naturally the word "disappeared" bursts out. What does it mean, someone asks? The word is multiplied many times by our mouths. It is repeated with the Ave Marias of the rosary. It embraces the word "impunity", our sense that the government is unwilling to take any responsibility for its actions. One woman, then another one, comes over to talk with us. Their children are also "disappeared", they want to see us again, to pray with us, even with diapers on their heads. People look on, listening to the rosary of the plaza. In the basilica, in front of the altar, some of the devoted women are taking Communion or praying for world peace. We are, in some way, the horrible worm that has wiggled out of a brilliant Argentina that is said to be "progressing". Toward what? Toward those graves without crosses. Towards the bottom of the river.

## "Heroic Night"

In November of 1977, Monsignor Antonio Jose Plaza, the archbishop of La Plata and a powerful ally of the dictatorship, announced that a "heroic night" would be held in the Plaza Moreno in front of the cathedral in La Plata. This was just before the World Soccer Cup was to be held in Buenos Aires; the celebration was designed to show that nothing bad was happening in Argentina.

The participants, who were all going to march together to a cathedral, were students from the Catholic schools in La Plata. We Mothers decided that we wanted to be there too, so we filtered ourselves into the group from the Marist College. We wore our new white kerchiefs, a step up from diapers, for the first time. It was an important act for us.

When the police saw us they started to follow us, but since we were all mixed in with the student group they didn't say a word. As we approached Plaza Moreno, the police began to surround us in an attempt to isolate our group. Then we began to pray, but as they all have so much fear of God, they let us pray. And we prayed "Our Fathers" and "Ave Marias" and the rosary, one after the other, until we got to the door of the cathedral. Once we had installed ourselves inside, the young people who were outside came in to see who we were. And we told them.

At midnight there were supposed to be festivities in the plaza, with guitar playing and singing and empanadas. But at this point a big group of students from the Catholic schools announced to Monsignor Plaza that they didn't want to play their guitars, and they didn't want to sing or eat empanadas outside in the plaza while there was so much pain and sorrow inside the cathedral.

And the young people all went home. The only ones who were left were us. We spent the night alone in the cathedral. At five in the morning many of the students came back to be with us for the early mass. And when Monsignor Plaza didn't say a word about the disappeared, we insulted him. Nobody understood why we did that—except for all those students who later went back to their homes and told everyone about us.

# CHAPTER 6

## DISCOVERING THE TRUTH

*Detectives*

The horrifying pattern of the repression of "subversives" continued and persuaded us that we should begin to be more organized in everything we did. At that time we mothers felt that the only way to strike back at this abusive regime was to become detectives, a kind of secret information service. Some of us would cover the jails, some would find out about the group of young people at the First Army Corps, and others kept making inquiries at the Ministry of the Interior.

Like hound dogs, each of us followed the trails of our children after they had been abducted. We found out the names of the kidnappers, identified police stations and concentration camps, spied on their death "transfers", found the cars the abductors had used and even discovered phonograph records that had been stolen from our children. Many of us mothers know who tortured our children and what they did to them with terrifying machines we could never have imagined. We know whether they tortured them with electric shocks and where, and how many days our children were hooded.

The best sources of information about our disappeared children were the very few prisoners who had been freed. They were the only ones who knew the truth, who might have seen our children or heard some rumors about their situation.

One day someone told us that the boy who ran the kiosk near the plaza had been a prisoner for a month before they let him go. Ten or fifteen mothers met together and, without thinking, we began hounding the boy. "Did you see so and so? Have you seen another so and so? Where are they? What are they doing to them?"

The boy wasn't a bad person, quite the contrary. He was just scared to death and he was afraid of the police who were keeping watch from across the street while fifteen women pursued him with questions. So he denied everything. He said that there was some confusion, that he had never been a prisoner. Our questioning continued and he finally had to close his kiosk for a few months.

We understood his panic because he was still under surveillance and he had to be very careful what he did if he didn't want to be beaten or perhaps imprisoned again. And yet, for us, that gift of people who had been freed was our only chance to learn something about our children.

One depressing side of all this were the cases of mothers we knew whose children were miraculously released. These women still lived in such a state of fear that they completely disappeared from our meetings, they stopped answering their telephones, and some of them even moved to another city. These women who had been our companions forgot all about those of us who were still struggling to find our children and denied us the information that their children might have brought us.

## Ferrer's Story

After a few months, when my strength was beginning to come back and I was finding a constructive outlet for my grief, another blow laid me flat: Humberto's mother was operated on for cancer. So now, added to all the dismal business about Jorge and my brother's death, I began making regular visits to the hospital. Curiously, I envied her in her morphine state. There were times when I wished I could sleep for a long, long time without knowing about anything—and then wake up to the world we used to have.

Humberto was spiritually destroyed; he just couldn't understand it all.

One day while I was at the hospital, a nurse came in and said that there was a woman out in the hall who wanted to see me. A neutral face was waiting for me at the end of the cold corridor. I didn't know the woman and she didn't introduce herself but only said "A man called Ferrer says he saw your son. He asked me to say that he wants to see you."

I went out and talked briefly with Ferrer in the hall, but he insisted that we meet him later in a bar in La Plata. Humberto and I went together to see him. He said he was an old schoolmate of mine. When I realized who he was it didn't seem possible that that kid I had played with in school, who was just my age, could have become the gray-haired man we were talking with.

"They took me to the Fifth Precinct station," Ferrer said very slowly. "I was accused of stealing a watch and under that pretext they held me for a few weeks, investigating. After a while they threw me into the collective cell. And it was jammed—you have no idea—sixty, seventy people on a cement floor, many of them hooded and bound with pieces of clothing. Do you want to know more?"

"Yes. I want to know. I want to know everything."

'"They were beaten up and bloody. And there was only a hole in the floor where we could relieve ourselves in front of everyone else. The water faucet was outside in the hall. And if the police guard felt like pulling the chain, he would flush it. If not, they left it all there for days—a hole full of the shit of seventy people. Kika, it was asphyxiating.

"After they stopped interrogating me and I felt a little better, I began to talk with some of the boys in that collective cell. All of them on their last legs. One boy came over to me and we began to talk in low voices so the guard wouldn't hear us. He said his name was Jorge and that he had just finished his studies in physics, that they had torn up his monograph on the laser and that he didn't have any other copies, that when he got out of prison he would have to put all his work together again. 'Everything that took me a year to do'."

"He also told me about what they did to him after they abducted him in February. The torture, the interrogations. Kika, there are things that you don't need to know. But yes, I know, you want to know everything."

"Later, at the end, Jorge cried. He called for his Mamita, he remembered a place in El Dique, the people selling sand there and the docks. As he cried, Jorge asked, "Has Uncle Warner died?" It was then that I realized: "Is your mother Kika Pastor?

"Then he smiled and stopped crying and he asked me to find you and to tell you what had happened to him. I talked to him about you and how we had gone to school together. I used my memory to invent you a little.

"Then Jorge embraced me and looked me straight in the eyes. 'If you should ever get out of here, tell Mama where I am. Tell her everything because she'll want to know. She always wants to know everything. And tell her to get me out.'"

We left the bar. Toto was walking in silence beside me. He said he wanted to go to the hospital to see his mother for a few minutes and then he and I would talk. I said I'd just be right there, walking around.

While I was walking, I kept repeating Ferrer's words. He had spoken so softly, without any hatred, with that frightening tranquility that comes with destroyed nerves— as if he still hadn't found his freedom or as if it would no longer do him any good, as if the electrodes of torture might have taken away his last grain of innocence.

Then I thought about the message from Jorge and I picked up my pace. My feet were running on their own and they knew their destiny. I entered the Fifth Precinct station—the sergeant at the door didn't dare stop me—and I went right into the commissioner's office. And I screamed, now that I knew that Jorge was there—tied up, without food or clothes, next to that well of shit. I screamed at each of the policeman, calling them assassins, degenerate criminals, who didn't deserve to live. I screamed that they were lying and that they knew that my son, Jorge Bonafini, was being held captive in a cell with seventy people, without food, without clothes—worse than an animal.

And as I screamed, I shouted all the dirty words I knew and the shout itself gave me the right and the strength to let every policeman in that place hear me. Perhaps even Jorge might hear me if he wasn't unconscious. I screamed until four policemen took me by the arm and used their weapons to shove me into the corner. Finally, the most brutish of the lot pushed me hard and said: "That's enough from you, you crazy old woman!"

I had nothing to do but leave. I would never be able to get my child back.

## Awful Truths

The hunt for bits of news was having miserable rewards. From one freed young man who agreed to talk with me, I learned that after my visit to the Fifth Precinct, after my talk with Ferrer, Jorge was punished. "A tremendous beating. By some miracle it didn't kill him."

How to understand such things. A man is beaten because his mother is frantic and is looking for him. Our sons pay for it because their mothers struggle to free them. What paths then are left to the mothers? We either had to stop fighting for our children, thereby risking their lives, or go on, even though our children might be punished for it.

Now only the will to know what was happening moved me, even though this almost inevitably implied that I would hear about scenes of extreme horror. And that is exactly what happened. Each new piece of news was worse than the last. When we thought that our sense of shock had been completely exhausted, we heard even more terrifying stories. The infinitely worse was possible: shackles, hoods, and finding out the significance of the word "submarine". All of this went far beyond the limits of our understanding or our tolerance.

But I still wondered—why that show of horror, the morbid invention of tortures? I am not able to speak of Jorge's body because I gave birth to him, I held him in my arms and I kissed his fat arms and his little white bottom and he took my milk until he became a person. And then those men came and they did to him what they did. To speak of the tortures to that body, whose human voice they forced to scream like an animal, is just turning the knife in the wound.

The truth is that if I should close my eyes and imagine that body covered all over with blood and bruises, I would feel a terrible shame. Because I would be seeing Jorge with another kind of nudity and to describe his torture would be to humiliate him, to repeat the torture, to make the violation all the worse. Why insult once again those bodies that had already been humiliated so many times in every imaginable way?

By late 1977 we felt that we could not retreat. If we had been resigned mothers (and there were such women, sitting on sofas by the front door in a sterile waiting game) it might have been possible. But now that we were beginning to know the truth and were armed with information, we couldn't hold ourselves back—even though the authorities made every attempt to shatter us and break up our growing movement.

# CHAPTER 7

## HORRENDOUS DAYS

*Azucena*

Azucena and I began to feel very close, perhaps because neither of us lived in Buenos Aires and because her husband, Pedro, was so like Humberto, even down to looking alike. I guess we just identified with one another. Our most significant bond was that she had a son and a daughter-in-law who had both been "disappeared".

The difficult situations of those days took all my concentration and really tested my brainpower; more than once Azucena fueled my energy. I observed her carefully; she was the master of quickness and shrewd intelligence. To me it was amazing that the creativity that she had used in an earlier job now had a completely new focus. Every day she would have some bright idea, some alternative plan that would increase the chances of succeeding in everything we were trying to do.

We all learned from Azucena. We wanted to be imbued with her spirit and that feeling of security she gave us that encouraged us to take small steps. We admired the independence with which she did things and her natural charisma—not the deceitful show of politicians, but

something that came from the strength of a person who argues on the side of truth.

Azucena would say "We have to read the newspapers carefully and cut out all the stories about important people who are coming to Argentina." So we clipped articles and then when any of those influential people came to Buenos Aires, we would find out where they were staying and install ourselves in their hotel and ask for interviews. We went all over—we, "the old women", tore all around the city.

Or Azucena would say "This week, concentrate on Cardinal Primatesta". And each of us would write her letter to Primatesta, just the way we wrote to every priest, to all the politicians and trade union leaders and journalists. There was not one important person whom we didn't flood with letters, written by hand, and, I'm sure, with mistakes, telling them the facts of our disappeared children.

## Letter to Videla

One day I even wrote a letter to Videla, the infamous leader of the junta. It doesn't seem pretentious to me—after all, he's the one responsible. I don't even care if people say it's a stupid thing to do, or, worse, that it's an act of suicide. It's something I just have to do.

Señor, President of the Republic:

I am also addressing the man, the person in the street, the husband, the son. Perhaps these lines may not reach you. If that should happen, the person who reads this letter and does not allow it to reach its destiny will have the remorse of not having fulfilled his duty as a citizen. If you do read it, I must tell you that it represents my sad grief as a mother and my pain as a citizen of a country where they say that no rights are being violated.

On the 8th day of February, at about one o'clock in the afternoon, in the name of the Army and the Combined Forces, they broke open the doors of my son's house, knocked him unconscious, covered him with a hood and took him away. But first they robbed him of his personal property and household goods.

Señor, my son is 26 years old, he is an exemplary child, a loving husband and an excellent student. Those are things that you can prove. He has his bachelor's degree and until now has been a student at the School of Exact Sciences of La Plata where he studies and works. Ever since that disastrous day, and despite the fact that he was taken away in the name of the Army, they have not given me any explanation. Señor, I believe that as a citizen I have the minimal right of finding my son. I don't believe that you govern a country where it would be so easy to make people disappear without anyone giving a reason for it. Even though everyone tells me not to write you and that it won't get any results, I go on believing in the people who govern and I request that you grant me an audience so that I can talk with you. Señor, President, I beg you, I implore you, I entreat you to receive me. I want you to explain to me this thing that is happening to so many of us Argentine mothers. I believe that, as President, you cannot ignore it. I write to you without any sense of diplomatic protocol. I don't know anything about all that. I don't understand it. The only thing I know how to do is to guide my pencil and, through my pencil to express my grief as a mother, my lack of power. Do you know what it is like to knock on every door for seventy-five days and find that the answer is always silence? I hope that silence may not also be your response.

Señora Hebe Pastor de Bonafini

## Suspicions

Sometimes, besides meeting on Thursdays in the Plaza de Mayo, we would work at Azucena's house in Sarandi. We would write letter after letter, and then we would just sit there thinking about more people we could go see or write. At night, if we finished late, Toto understood if I thought I should spend the night at her house.

One night after dinner, when we were having tea and talking about the Plaza, her husband, Pedro, suddenly came out with a disturbing observation.

"There's something about Gustavo that I don't like. He's always hanging around you, Azucena, and asking you what you plan to do over the week-end and where you live."

"But, Pedro," I injected "he's alone and he's looking for his brother and his parents live somewhere outside of Buenos Aires. Just imagine. It's logical that he should seek out our leader. It's as though he saw Azucena as a mother."

Azucena herself kept on saying that with his lovely face that boy, Gustavito, couldn't hurt a fly. But Pedro didn't agree. "I don't know why, but I don't like his type at all."

After Pedro went to bed, Azucena and I stayed up talking in front of the stove in the golden candlelight. I didn't feel that Azucena was just my friend. I felt about her as I would a sister.

"Which of our children will appear first?"

"Yours, Azucena, I'm sure. You're the one who does the most work."

"No, they'll free Jorge first, I'm certain. No. They'll free all three."

## Mother's Day Notice

One Thursday, late in **1977**, Azucena arrived at the Plaza and we could see that she was really excited. She had just gotten the addresses of Amnesty International and the Organization of American States. "First we have to write individual letters and then we can do joint letters." Then she said that we had to start collecting money among ourselves to buy space in some of the newspapers. For a notice. "It's like a paid ad where a person can say whatever he likes—as long as they let you, of course. Now that they've taken our children, the best idea would be to publish the notice on Mother's Day, our day of no celebration. And if all goes well, and we can raise enough money, we'll have another notice on the 10th of December—Human Rights Day."

So we all got busy and wrote the notice on notebook paper. Then we carried it over to the offices of the newspaper, *La Nación*. They took one look at it and said, "No, Señoras. We can't do it handwritten like that. It has to be typed."

Well we didn't have an office and, at that point, we didn't have a typewriter. But luckily we found some people at the Ministry of the Interior who offered to type up our notice if we would just entertain their two bosses while they did it. The employees typed the notice and we took it back to the newspaper office.

Then there was a new hurdle. All we wanted was to have them print the names of our children who had disappeared. But the newspaper, for some mysterious reason we didn't understand at the time, required the identities of the mothers. And they asked that a Certificate of Domicile accompany each of our names. That meant that we had to go to the police station and explain why we needed the certificate. The junta's chain of information worked without flaws, right down the line. They never needed to go looking for us; we were perfectly established now, as individuals at given addresses. The worst of it was that, in the beginning, we didn't even realize what was happening.

Finally, after we had complied with all their conditions, we took the notice back to the newspaper office. Our notice came out in *La Nación*. on October 15th, Mothers' Day in Argentina.

## Waiting for Raúl

On December 6, 1977 I was standing in my kitchen in City Bell, stirring a pot of stew and worrying about Raúl. He had lost his buoyant happiness and his wild ways. He didn't joke around any more and had become pensive and fearful. And he no longer had much time for his blessed snakes.

I know he tried not to think about himself, but it was inevitable. These days the university was a hostile place. Many of his friends had been disappeared—and now his brother. The only way for him to survive those blows was to fight back. He had always been active in the labor unions so this was the path he chose. I couldn't tell him to stop working there or not to be involved in union activities, but I was scared to death.

I was also thinking about Alejandra as I stood there stirring the pot. About how she hadn't had the chance to have a normal childhood, at least not for this past year. She'd lost her grandmother and her uncle—and now she was waiting, day-by-day, for Jorge to return.

I was also remembering earlier, happier times this year. On Mother's Day, Alejandra and Raúl had showered me with presents—enough to make me cry a little. I had had a kind of perverse pleasure in seeing our notice in the newspaper with the list of all our disappeared children. Publishing it in a prestigious morning newspaper must have shaken up all those incredulous, innocent, people who trusted our government and shut their eyes and their Persian blinds—all those people who denied that anything was happening in Argentina.

But mostly I was worrying about Raúl while I stirred that pot. He said he'd be back late and I had planned to leave him something to eat. But sleep was overcoming me and I couldn't stay awake any longer.

## The Truth Registers

The next day I waited and waited. Finally I call Maria Elena.

"Maria Elena, listen. Where is he? He didn't come here to sleep. It's two in the afternoon and he hasn't called."

"Hold on, Hebe. We still aren't sure what happened." I knew all too well her tone of voice; she was trying to control herself. She had used that same voice to speak about Jorge. I shouted at her not to give me the run-around. She finally told me.

"Hebe, I'm sorry I didn't tell you right away, but I wanted to wait a little longer to see what the union would do. They haven't done a thing. Yesterday there was a meeting of the workers, in a private house, in Berazategui. Hebe, they came in cars and took away six of them. What are we going to do?"

I didn't even sit down. I just stayed at the sink, scrubbing my hands. I realized that all this repression had nothing to do with retaliation against me. It was retaliation against the world, against life—the government's response to an unstable world. Those monsters running loose in our country were capable of dragging off Raúl as if he were nothing, a wretched cog in some wheel. But he was a man. They weren't able to understand a person who was studying ecology and had two jobs because he needed the money. And they had no idea that he loved insects and that one afternoon he had even filled our patio with snakes and crocodiles. But for now I had to forget all those things, or rather I had to convert those thoughts into pure action, into a search, into rage.

Toto had listened to my end of the conversation and had gone off by himself. I found him out in the backyard, by the clothes line, sitting there on a box. He was just looking off into empty space with his mouth half open and petting our dog. He raised his face and looked at me. His eyes were turned inward, as if he were remembering the first nightmare of Jorge, a nightmare that now, almost nine months later, we would have to relive.

He didn't say a word. Then he got up and went to Alejandrita's room. "Come on, sweetheart. Get dressed. We're going to take you to grandma's. No, nothing's happened. It's just a routine thing."

My friend Lydia went with me on the train. We traveled in silence; I didn't want to start crying until I knew what was happening. Berazategui isn't far away, but the trip seemed interminable. I had a paper with the address in my hand. It had become a tiny ball.

We knocked at the door of that house where they'd had the meeting. Nobody answered. A neighbor insisted that the Señora was there because she'd just come back from the police station where she'd been brought in as a witness. We knocked again—this time with our fists. With the chain still set, the woman's face appeared. She looked at us and said yes, they had taken the union men away in cars, yesterday afternoon. "But don't bother looking for them any more because they killed them all. And calm down."

That woman, who is called Carmen and who lives at Covadonga and 2 de Mayo showed me her enormous capacity for cruelty. She is yet another name on my list of thoroughly contemptible people. We left the house and knew that once again we would have to go through the whole bureaucratic rigmarole of the habeas corpus.

A month later we learned that on December 7, 1977 Raúl had been taken to the Police Station at Berazategui, the place where that woman had testified.

## From "I" to "We"

With Jorge, everything had been desperation—a blow to the head like the one they had given him. The day I learned about Raúl, that desperation disappeared, like Raúl. It was replaced by a profound sadness, deep within me, a sadness that didn't seem like anything else I had ever known.

I was calm for a few hours, just looking off into space. I let time pass. It seemed endless. To imagine Raúl, the gadabout, shut up for hours, to see his clothes in his chest of drawers, his books on entomology. Sadness drained me of my strength.

But then I said to myself, isn't that just what they're looking for with their repetition of hideous crimes? Don't they just want to demonstrate to me their infinite power? So. I had to come out of my consuming sorrow and transform my grief into intelligence. And be on the attack.

Raúl's story, from the very beginning, uprooted the word "I" from my thinking and was converted into a "we" that changed my life. Raúl was important to me, and so was Jorge. But the other children who had been taken away were my "disappeared" as well. We are all of us together, I thought, and we have to keep on, even though tomorrow they may beat us into dust—all of us—our husbands, even the mothers in our group. We have to take a stand, to decide if we will fight them or not. And perhaps there will be no turning back.

## "Drug Operation"

The following day I went into Buenos Aires to be with the Mothers.

"Raúl isn't anywhere . . . ," I burst out as soon as someone opened the door to Nora's house. The other mothers were all there. "Hush, Hebe, don't say a word . . . ."

Azucena put her arms around me and then gently put her hand over my lips.

There was general confusion in the room. Someone was crying, another person was writing something. Azucena was getting me some tea, someone else asked for details about Raúl. Everything seemed frenzied, disordered. I sat down with my cup of tea to listen.

Maria del Rosario was clearly nervous but she began telling me what had happened. The day before, Thursday, December 8, after marching in the Plaza, the mothers had gone to the Church of Santa Cruz because they wanted to collect money for the notice to appear in the paper on December 10th. (With all the business of searching for Raúl, I hadn't been able to go.) As the mothers entered the church they became aware that strange-looking men surrounded it.

"Right away I mentioned this to Beatriz. But she said that she hadn't noticed them. Just before Communion, the bag for collecting money was furtively passed around. Suddenly Gustavo appeared. 'What are you doing here?' I asked Gustavito, the blond boy whose brother was missing. 'You're the only young man here—you run the most risk.' But Gustavo said that he wanted to be with us on such an important day."

"After the money had been collected he said that he was going out for a few minutes to get some fresh air. Beatriz and I went out behind him because we needed to leave early. But we didn't get to more than the corner."

Maria del Rosario went on telling the story. "Beatriz and I wanted to speak to our friends who were also leaving—the people from the Relatives of the Detained and Disappeared group who had been working with us. That was when that we saw the men on the corner. They were carrying weapons and they suddenly began attacking us.

"Drug operation!" the men shouted as they assaulted Maria and Esther. They beat them; the women screamed and resisted. Another man grabbed me and pushed me up against the wall. 'Quiet down, you crazy old woman, if you don't want to come with us!" he shouted at me and left me there, motionless."

"Then a bunch of cars appeared and they threw the women in the cars—our friends and the people from the Relatives group. All of them had been beaten. The men let Beatriz and me go and we went back into the church. We don't know if they took Gustavo away too." [EN-J: Astiz]

"But that's terrible!" I exclaimed. "We have to go look for our friends."

Azucena was quick to answer. "We called the 20th Precinct Station from the church and they said they had nothing to report. But anyway, there are already people looking for them." Azucena's voice was serene, but firm. "Our friends were kidnapped because they were collecting money for this notice. Tomorrow is Human Rights Day; we absolutely have to get them out."

And then I started wondering out loud how we could go on if as soon as we turned around they beat us up and dragged away our children and our friends. In that instant, I had the first real consciousness of what and who we were fighting, of the dimensions of our enemy. I felt that they were capable of doing away with all of us, with everyone, so there wouldn't be a relative or a friend left of those first people who had been detained.

"But, Hebe, you mustn't think of that now," Azucena said. "Please. Now we have to concentrate on how to write this blessed notice." We added the new names to the list of disappeared: the other mothers, Esther de Careaga, the French nun, Alice Domon, Maria Ponce, and the people from the relatives group: Angel Auad, Patricia Oviedo, Eduardo Horrane, Raquel Bulit. We didn't add Gustavo's name because no one had seen them put him in a car. Had he been taken him away or did he somehow save himself?"

I closed my eyes. I didn't want to let myself be completely disheartened. One of the mothers clapped as we finished passing the notice around. The whole situation was macabre. Our happiness was sinister, but it reflected the reality of those days. Azucena triumphantly announced that writing that notice for the newspaper represented a tremendous victory for us.

At last I felt that I wanted to go on living. As long as I was still living my children would not be dead. Nobody would be able to kill them. Ever.

## Human Rights Day

After our meeting Azucena and I went to the bus station together.

"Azucena, you amaze me. You're always thinking up something. I wish I could learn to do things like that. At times it seems to me that not even a hundred dictatorships could keep you down. How do you do it?"

"You don't want to know, Hebe," she says. "I learned everything I know from the people they took away from me."

I have brought Azucena a present and before we each get on our buses to go home I give it to her. It's a briefcase. Azucena says that she's also brought something for me. She pulls a piece of paper out of her pocketbook. It's a poem by Mario Benedetti; I'm very pleased. "I learned to read poetry with Jorge," I tell her and she smiles, happy.

"Tomorrow I'm going to get up a little late because it's Saturday," she tells me "and first thing I'm going over to the kiosk to buy the newspaper. I can hardly wait to see how our notice will look."

Azucena watches me as I get on my bus. I choose a window near where she's standing and we keep on talking right up to the last minute. "Thanks for the poem," I shout as the bus pulls away. The last thing I see is that open, tender smile, and her short, plump arm waving to me.

On Human Rights Day, December 10, 1977, Azucena Villaflor de DeVincente walked with short, agile steps to the kiosk on the corner by her house in Sarandi. She was never seen again, but her spirit and her strength live in us all.

## Renewed Determination

Returning to the Plaza de Mayo after Azucena's disappearance took one of the major efforts of my life. Riding in on the bus I tried to pull myself together. I was hoping to make some sense of all the dreadful things that had just happened. The only thing I could come up with at that moment was the memory of something Azucena had said in one of the churches—between the "Our Fathers" we used to disguise our meetings. "To let down our guard, Hebe, is to permit impunity, to permit the guilty to escape accountability."

As I walked towards the Plaza I was overwhelmed by that hostile place, so full of uniforms and bludgeons and people who appeared to be completely indifferent to what was happening in Argentina. Everything in the Plaza seemed to emphasize the great void left by Azucena's disappearance. Wasn't her experience a foreboding of what would happen to each one of us? For the moment our victories were only gathering losses; our effectiveness was being measured by new disappearances.

As I approached the Plaza I could only see a few defeated women there. All they apparently wanted at that moment was a truce with the police. Somehow it seemed to me that if we let them take away any more of us mothers it would be an open confession that we had done something

wrong. But these new acts of police aggression against the mothers should tell us how we ought to respond. I now became convinced that these latest acts of terrorism should persuade us to gather our strength and continue our struggle.

Once in the Plaza, I could see that our march of silent protest was about to begin again. I crossed the Plaza and, with new determination, I joined the march.

# CHAPTER 8

## GAINING VISIBILITY

*Recovery*

After Azucena was taken away by the secret police, the vacuum she left was gradually filled with new strength. In the midst of the terror, of the lost children who every day seemed further away, a little laughter grew timidly. Although it sounds brutal, because it is, we found a certain happiness, the paradoxical happiness that comes from all of us supporting one another.

Knowing that it would be a hard year for us and that we would have to confront increased persecution, we felt obliged to be in church more than ever. "Hail Mary, full of grace (Monday at 5:30. We'll meet at the Ideal Coffee Shop) the Lord is with thee . . .". That's what our rosaries were like, messages squeezed into the prayer; messages that were passed along the bench and inevitably became distorted. That meant we often went to the wrong place, some of us ending up in one café, the rest of us in others.

We had energy and a lot of commitment, but as spies I have to admit that we were a calamity. Our security system was transparent. If we wanted to disguise a meeting place when threatening ears were close, we used childish signals. The Roses or the Carnations Café, instead of the Violets; the Little Boat instead of The Frigate. No one would have to invest much time to figure out the place we'd be meeting.

## Circulating Money

One day, someone had a bright idea for how we could spread our message. "Let's write on paper money."

We began by writing on small bills, at first on 100 peso ones. Over the face of General San Martín we wrote in very clear letters "So-and-so, disappeared on the x day at the intersection of y and z streets. He has been kidnapped by . . . ." One of our husbands suggested that that was a good excuse for their wives to spend money quickly. But the system delivered its fruits.

Within a couple of months all of La Plata did nothing but talk about the mysterious bills with the writing on them. But you had to be very careful about putting the bills into circulation. They were passed around half folded up, between other bills. They were effective because whoever got one wanted to get rid of it just as fast as he could. (That was the theory of the woman who thought it up.) The bills circulated rapidly and at times they even came back to the people who had written them. The green grocers were talking about the money, and so were the butcher and the florist. Sometimes they smiled when they got one, just so they wouldn't raise any suspicion.

But the government's capacity to burn this money with abandon (a crime for anyone else under the Civil Code) was such that they got a lot of bad press on top of everything else. We began to write on large bills. We knew that after a while people would stop paying any attention to our bills. That was something we had foreseen. And so it was, because people also began to make jokes about them. ("I just happened to get another So-and-so 500"). We stopped writing on bills. But it didn't matter, we'd think of something else.

## Marching in La Plata

Gradually I began to put myself in charge of our connections with the mothers of the disappeared in La Plata. There were already a tremendous number of them. Many weren't able to, or didn't dare to, go in to the Plaza de Mayo in Buenos Aires on Thursdays, so we decided to march around the Plaza San Martín in La Plata every Wednesday.

## Letter To Primatesta

The Mothers kept up a steady stream of letters to people who we thought might make a difference in our attempts to tell the truth about the disappearances. On May 2, 1978 I wrote a letter to the influential Cardinal Primatesta protesting his non-appearance before a group of mothers. It said in part:

"What sadness! What dismay! Seventy-four of us Mothers returned from San Miguel, soaked from rain, grief and tears. Our Cardinal didn't receive us, he didn't give us the benediction that we had so hoped for. Some of us left home at 4:30 in the morning to get to San Miguel by 10— and yet our pastor didn't have time, not one single minute to see us . . . . Our bishops have a pact of silence with Videla."

## Postcards

One day at our Mothers meeting Adelina was the last to arrive. As she opened the door we could see she was amused, almost tempted to smile. "Wait 'til they see!" she said and we all wondered what she was talking about. "It took me all morning, but it was worth it!" She sat down nervously on the edge of the chair, opened her purse and pulled out a card with an assortment of colored letters that said, **In argentina children are assassinated.**

"What do you think?" Adelina asked, but we still didn't understand.

Then she explained. All during 1978, at the time when some people had a campaign to discredit our country, the magazine *Para Tí* had launched an offensive of postcards praising the Argentine government. These postcards were inserted in the magazine and the editor urged readers to send them abroad with messages such as **In argentina all children go to school. Our country has eradicated violence.** He specifically suggested sending them to people like Senator Edward Kennedy and organizations such as Amnesty International.

Adelina had patiently cut out each one of the original letters and rearranged them in sentences that expressed exactly the opposite meaning. Each card had taken more than two hours to do, but the result was terrific. (Poor editor—if only he had known what those United States senators were receiving.) There was applause for Adelina's ingenuity.

That same afternoon we all began the frenetic activity of cutting out the letters and making the cards. By nightfall we had cut up a good many cards, had "corrected" their deceitful message and had begun circulating our own message around the world. When *Para Tí* finally got wind of what we were doing they stopped printing the cards.

## Combating Repression

For several months we had been creating slogans and rallying cries. They just broke loose from our silent circling of the pyramid in the center of the Plaza. But for the month of May in 1978 we kept quiet. The police waited punctually at three every Thursday and charged whenever they saw more than three women together. We fought them off as long as possible. They caught us in one corner and we shifted to the other corner. They took us out of one flowerbed and, after we'd gone around the block, we turned up beside another one. The game of cat and mouse that exasperated them so much had, for us, the almost symbolic objective of occupying the space around the pyramid, the center of the plaza. From there people would see us better.

But we were completely helpless in combating some of the junta's acts of repression. On the 25th of May, in the afternoon, military forces abducted a group of women in a pastry shop. One of them was Maria Elena Bugnone, Jorge's wife. Of that group of women no one ever returned.

## The World Cup

By that May, the frenzy of the approaching World Cup was heating up. Propaganda flowing from the useless office of some lofty priest promoted the idea of "cleansing the country very thoroughly of disturbing elements before the first tourists set foot in Argentina. 'Our country is going to demonstrate to the world its capacity for recuperation'." Translated, this meant that the government would exterminate dissension at any cost.

In the same way the government put up walls to hide the misery of poverty and moved entire shantytowns, they also needed to cover up all of us mothers because we were regarded as a stain on the country. We knew that the authorities were afraid that too many eyes would converge on Argentina for those women to go right on making a big hullabaloo and broadcasting their demands. But we also knew that with the World Cup the country would be full of tourists and people representing the media from all over the world. It was then that I put a question to our group:

"How do we take advantage of those TV cameras for our own cause, so we can ask about our children and start a juicy scandal?"

"But we don't know how to talk very well, Hebe. We know how to keep house and we've learned how to do the paperwork, but what are we going to answer if they ask us something in English?"

"It's easy, Clarita," piped up one of the mothers. "You look at the journalist and you say 'We want our children back. We want them to tell us where they are'."

June 1st at 3 o'clock—the opening day of the World Cup. It began with the flutter of Argentine flags and confetti thrown from office windows. This just showed the indifference of Argentines who didn't want to know anything about death and preferred to celebrate that mad fiesta that suggests power to them, that stuffs them full with their four TV channels until they have indigestion or are completely brain-washed.

We women, meanwhile, worked at spreading the news about our group. We sent hundreds of letters to foreign politicians and we sought interviews with different world TV networks. Those men listened to us carefully and some of them became indignant. They all considered us good journalistic material. We had made it.

While local TV channels are showing the euphoric flight of hundreds of doves in the stadium, most of the journalists are with us in the Plaza de Mayo, covering the reverse side of the Argentine coin: "Boycotting the World Cup". A superior restrains the police, so used to charging us without needing any orders, just as we were waiting for their attack. All this to the jubilation of Dutch TV that decided to send pictures of the Mothers instead of the simultaneous shots of the opening. The TV networks interview us; they cover our march around the pyramid. We extend bridges to the outside world through the words of the correspondents who are covering the championship.

## Conference on Cancer

As if it wasn't enough for the government with the World Cup, we got additional attention when the International Congress on Cancer met in Buenos Aires. We went to that conference and spoke out and the doctors listened. Three days later two doctors came to give us support in our march in the Plaza. They wore their credentials hung around their neatly tailored suits and no one was able to touch them. The Plaza was taken over by the police; the doctors just stepped out to the front of the line, defying the police.

One of the mothers, protected by the doctors, shouted at the police: They took our children alive; we want them back alive. She repeated it and the rest of us took up the chant. **They took our children alive; we want them back alive.** Minutes later the marching was dissolved and we lost ourselves in the Avenida de Mayo. But another rallying cry had just been born. It wasn't anything, and yet it was everything. It succeeded in synthesizing our emotions; it denounced the junta. That chant itself had aroused us and we think that possibly it awakened some complacent passerby in his mad world of dollars and soccer goals.

## Trip Abroad

At last the Mothers were beginning to have some visibility, and to incite the concerted interest of international human rights groups. Before we knew it a trip was organized for a few of us to travel abroad.

We would be going to Washington, D. C. and then to Rome, Italy—to see the Pope! The trip had been arranged so quickly that it all seemed unreal. We divided up the expenses among several of the mothers, with the three of us who would go paying a little more. We also wrote dozens

of letters to people in the countries we would visit, telling them that we were on our way. We were pretty well organized but all the same, it was a little scary. We knew we were traveling into completely unknown territory.

The day to leave had arrived and my bags were packed: three skirts, all ironed, some pullovers, a topcoat I had borrowed because I knew that fall in the United States can be cold, shoes wrapped up in a nylon bag just the way Mama had taught me.

I looked at the topcoat that was already on top of my suitcase. Alejandra, wearing her best dress, was ready to go to the airport with me. I took a last turn around the house. Everything was in place.

For us to leave Argentina with the purpose of denouncing the repression in Argentina was undoubtedly a major crime in the eyes of the junta. There is no dictatorship that lasts without good public relations, and we were about to destroy some of the image of normalcy that the junta had tried so hard to convey to the outside world. We knew that making this trip to speak out against the Argentine dictatorship would be worth much more than the protests of hundreds of exiles.

We three mothers, Elida Galetti, Maria del Rosario and I, traveled first to Washington. We brought with us a list of addresses, but we didn't have any prearranged interviews. Nor experience. But, yes indeed, we certainly had a whole lot of fear. Was it really possible that our trip had escaped the junta's notice? As we were leaving we were afraid that every official we encountered was someone who might cause us trouble.

But we took off safely and finally the plane landed in Washington. I was now able to divide my worrying between losing the coat I had borrowed and trying to picture that "friend of a friend of a friend" who would be waiting for us in the arrival lounge. He turned out to be a very tall, strong, swarthy man who was wearing dark glasses.

"They've captured us, Hebe, I'm sure. They've captured us," said Maria del Rosario in one breath while she tugged on my sleeve.

"I'm Mario," said the very serious man.

"Documents, please," the three of us burst out almost at the same time, in an intuitive reminder of the junta.

"What??!" Mario said as he let out a big laugh. "We only carry our drivers' licenses here," he added. He showed us his and we saw that it actually bore the same name he'd just given us.

First of all Mario took us to have a coffee. As soon as he removed his dark glasses we stopped being afraid of him. He asked us where we wanted to go. "To the State Department," we answered. We had been so battered in our own country, but now we were being transformed into citizens of the world, into women who felt sure of themselves.

We could see the beautiful gardens of Washington as we rode along in the car, but we weren't interested in anything that would distract us from our mission. Our tour of Washington was limited to the public buildings and the homes of those people who were putting us up and driving us around. We met with the small but active colony of exiles who were spreading the word about the atrocities in Argentina; we also met with a group from Amnesty International—the first ones to make a list of the disappeared with the dates of their disappearance.

"We are the Mothers of the disappeared," said Maria del Rosario energetically. "From Buenos Aires, Argentina. We have come because of the human rights situation in our country." And immediately we would be in the presence of the secretary of Edward Kennedy or of some presidential advisor.

One of the Senators talked to us about his sons. So I told him about Muzzioli and the anchovies in brine, because I was far from home and needed a solid point of reference. That past of mine, so distinct and beloved, defined me better than any piece of paper ever could have.

Simplicity and directness seemed to be the miraculous keys to the most difficult doors. A combination of our self-confidence and the fact that we came without a translator, plus the silencing effect of our obvious innocence, led us to the offices of principal legislators. They listened and were interested. What I mean is that they seemed sincere in their concern, they took notes, they offered to introduce us to other people we should see. And they kept repeating to us that the important thing was to keep up our pressure on the junta.

With almost the same speed that we went from one office to another, we traveled from Washington to New York. ("If Azucena could see us now, Hebe!"—But Azucena was with us.) New contacts, interviews with journalists. We took advantage of the telephone numbers and addresses we had been given, and each call brought us together with other people who were concerned about human rights.

We spent an evening talking with a priest from Tibet House, a Christian group that offered housing to visitors who otherwise had no place to stay. The priest there was taken by surprise by our stories. He could hardly imagine that the regime in Argentina could be doing such atrocious things with impunity. And where were we planning on going next, he asked us.

"To see the Pope."

Wasn't the Pope the one who continued to be the arbiter of all the major conflicts in this world? We imagined that with a couple of phone calls he would have the power to slow down the arrests. The priest at Tibet House listened in amazement. And then he said, "I don't think you'll get to see him, but the officials at the Vatican will get you interviews with important people."

Of course, none of this deterred us from wanting to see the Pope. We said goodbye and he gave us his blessing.

In Rome we really had to count our pennies. Our hosts put us up in an empty apartment close to a plaza with marble steps. We looked at all those beautiful old buildings out of the corners of our eyes as we went to different interviews, some sessions of the Parliament, a brief interview with the Minister of Foreign Relations and, as he defined it, "a clandestine meeting" with Prime Minister Sandro Pertini. This was all part of our frenetic race against the clock and the calendar—as well as our pocketbooks—that were telling us that we couldn't spend much more time in Rome.

Jorge would have to understand that this time the Pope was too busy to see us. But the Argentine Cardinal, Eduardo Pironio, listened and he promised to speak to the Pope personally and to follow up on our concerns. "The Pope will be in touch with the situation," he assured us, and a priest high in the Jesuit hierarchy also promised us his support.

The trip had been a success. They had promised us to keep on the pressure. Now it was a question of returning to Argentina, very carefully, on tiptoes.

On the plane, flying back to Latin America, we just sat in silence. The air itself was a country without dictators and we didn't want the trip to end. Contemplating the whole business of immigration control in Buenos Aires made us feel extremely nervous.

"Maybe we shouldn't be so worried," I said. "We've

seen all those important people; I don't think they'd dare touch us now. Anyway, I have our pictures taken with Cardinal Pironio and the one with Senator Kennedy—so they'll give us some respect. Now . . ." Maria del Rosario grabbed my hand and I took hold of her arm. Trembling, with our eyes closed, we felt the airplane touch down in Argentina.

And then the complications began. One of our bags had gotten lost (translation: it was being gone through by the police) and another suitcase was being rifled (they turned it upside down looking for papers.) Our handbags were searched as if we were drug traffickers. (They found the photographs. Silence.)

Things finally got resolved with immigration control and to my great happiness I saw the faces of my family. Alejandra, Humberto and Mama. They all shouted at me, and minutes later we embraced. They seemed in good shape—not at all under-nourished. As soon as we got into our car I began to tell them how it had all been.


The truth is that for women like us who had always been confined to doing things in the family and only knew second-hand how the real world worked, it was very hard to understand all the formalities that we had observed on our trip. At times the ways of this new world almost seemed perverse to us. From El Dique to Rome was not only a great distance in kilometers; in reality that world was as far away as the moon. But, to our surprise, we had managed to change money, cope with the language, and talk with dignitaries with complete naturalness. Now that we had done this we considered everything that happened on the trip as our apprenticeship. I was learning, but without being overwhelmed. Behind this lasting discovery was always my guiding motive: finding out about the children who were no longer here—who had disappeared.

## Association Office

After our trip to the United States and Italy, we had the real challenge of deciding whether we were going to continue being a group of tireless, well-intentioned mothers, or whether we wanted to give deeper meaning to our work of searching for our children. We had to decide whether we would surrender the Plaza to the forces of the junta or whether we would have something to show for all our efforts. We felt that after working for two years, and finally beginning to see some results, we deserved more visibility. For one thing, we reasoned that even though we had been disappointed in the outcome, just having been able to persuade the Organization of American States' Commission on Human Rights to visit Argentina the following year should count for quite a lot in giving our group "respectability".

One of our problems was that we always met in public spaces. Now even the lowliest officials in the province knew our addresses and identification numbers. The junta didn't need any encouragement to repress people in those days and our twenty signatures on the newspaper ads and our weekly processions around the Plaza de Mayo put us in constant danger.

Although we had been identified as a group from the very beginning, we realized that if we put our names together as a single organization we would no longer be just mothers opposed to a government but an entity that wouldn't have to rely on a single individual to function. Also having an association would help us to recruit the support of some mothers who might feel better if they had an official organization backing them. That was what other groups who were defending human rights in Argentina had done. Quite honestly, we were afraid that if we didn't stick together legally, everything that had cost us so much effort would fall to pieces.

On the 14th of May 1979, we met at the home of Angelica Mignone and created the Association of the Mothers of the Plaza de Mayo. The Association was legally registered on August 22 of that year. These were two big steps for us.

We didn't have to invent a name; the people who had seen us during our processions around the plaza had already given it to us. We elected a group to lead us, a Commission of Eleven, and this gave us another boost. It made us feel different, very strong. Now we were something more than individual, desperate mothers who only rose up in protest. Now we had something, a name that belonged to us and something to which we could belong.

Someone said, "Now we need a president and vice president. They proposed Maria Adela and me. I always seem to end up by accepting challenges and responsibilities, so I responded immediately, almost without weighing the consequences. A good part of my reaction was motivated by the urgency of the whole business and by my overflowing energy that continued to take the place of my giving up. It was also in response to the stories of freed prisoners who felt more comfortable talking to an association. I felt that to search for our children was the only way to continue being a mother. But accepting the presidency also had, I can't deny it, a little bit of my old lack of humility that Humberto never stopped calling to my attention.

With the exception of a small number of Mothers who were professors and professionals, the majority of us were, for the first time, confronting the necessity of dealing systematically with important papers. Most of our files were quite disorganized—we simply hadn't realized that we were going to need an office. Up until then our only meeting places had been coffee shops and churches and each other's homes. We were like snails.

As soon as we had formed the Association we sent out letters all over the world—and we began to get answers in return. One of the letters came from some women in Holland who had formed a support group for the Mothers. They wondered how we could manage to do our work if we always had to carry on our business in public places and didn't have any mailing address. They said that this might have been all right in the beginning, but that now we should get ourselves established. And, they added, "If you would accept a donation from us, you could rent or buy an office."

The Commission of Eleven had been discussing the idea of an office for a long time and it was still going on when one day, quite by surprise, a check (their donation) arrived. It was only a simple piece of paper, but it was made out in our name—the Association of the Mothers of the Plaza de Mayo—for $25,000!

Right away it changed things for us. It gave us the possibility of growing, of taking on new projects that would be vital to us. We wasted no time in finding ourselves an office. We were beginning to have a sense of solidarity with people around the world.

## The Organization of American States (OAS) Visits Argentina

On September 7, 1979 the OAS Commission on Human Rights began to meet here in Argentina. Less than a year earlier we had initiated the visit, in fact, demanded it, with letters and in person when we were the United States. When they came to Buenos Aires we got an audience with the Commission on the very first day of their investigation and we talked with them every day after that. One day we asked to have all of the Mothers come before the Commission and

they let all hundred and fifty of us into the hall. We made accusations, we gave interviews.

But the problem was that the junta used lots of fanfare to try to convince the OAS that the Argentine people were perfectly happy and that no one knew anything about any disappeared people. Or maybe, and this is even worse, the junta tried to persuade the OAS that the disappeared were not important. The junta and its military officers were shrewd in their handling of the Human Rights Commission. It tried hard to fool the Commission into believing that everything was normal in Argentina. For example, during the OAS visit to the Naval Mechanics School (ESMA) the prisoners were taken to Tigre in the River Plata for a week, and everything was cleaned up, spic and span, in the building where there had been such horrendous torture. Earlier the junta had tried this same kind of deception when the Red Cross visited the 8th Commissary in La Plata.

When they left, the OAS Commission said that they would need to stay in permanent contact with us and they gave us some new addresses and the firm promise of a further investigation. But after they left our spirits dissolved in a feeling of great uneasiness and the fear of reprisals by the junta.

We had had such high hopes. The coming of the OAS had been really important to us. We believed that it would make a significant change; we felt that something was going to happen. But absolutely nothing happened because it was only a whitewash and the junta just killed more people and the terror actually got worse. [EN-K: OAS Visit]

# CHAPTER 9

## WORD FROM PRISONS

*Report on Jorge*

One day a young man came to me saying that he had something to tell me about Jorge. He asked for a coffee. He stirred in some sugar and then was quiet for a moment, just looking at the coffee. Then he lifted his eyes. More than a year after Jorge's kidnapping, this boy was the second witness to come to me—the only one after Ferrer, the only other released prisoner who had wanted to talk.

And he talked. He was almost twenty-five years old but his fuzzy cheeks made him look like some young kid. It was strange that torture and so much pain hadn't left more of a mark on him. His body seemed whole, with no scars, even healthy. Only his hands trembled a little—incessantly.

First he spoke of himself: they had taken him to a place called "La Quinta" (the 5th Precinct) around the middle of 1977. "That was a dungeon, Señora, I swear it." I asked him what they did to him. "Señora, better ask what they didn't do to us . . . ." And he recounted everything, very seriously, almost with shame. His hands were still shaking. He had seen my son there, but he never managed to talk with him. He didn't even know his name. "And now you're going to wonder why they let me go! Even if it makes me feel a little ashamed to be released, Señora, I swear it, I didn't do anything special to be selected."

"I'm not going to wonder anything. I only want you to tell me!"

Then he said that everything was madness. It was only madness the way they let some people go free and beat others to a pulp in interrogation. He had been released "because of his pretty face", a guard had said mockingly. That had been the same day that others, my son Jorge among them, were taunted about going before the firing squad." Don't think that there's any logic or justice involved in what they do. "It's almost a question of luck."

"Tell me about Jorge."

"Well, I don't really know anything. I only remember that they had begun to leave him more or less alone. It's a blessing when it seems they've forgotten someone. But one afternoon they came looking for him; they brought him out on his hands and knees. 'We heard that your old lady is making noise,' they yelled at him. 'Now you'll see.' And they took him to the interrogation room and they beat him and they shouted at him that 'it wasn't at all surprising that he had turned out twisted, with a crazy mother who even came there to yell at us' and they began to beat him again. Between the blows and the shouts, there was a tremendous uproar. At last they let him talk and your son yelled back at them: 'My mother is going to see the Pope and get me out.' And they beat him again until he was silent.

## Fattening Up Roberto

One day in 1980 one of the Grandmothers of the
Plaza de Mayo received an anonymous letter from a
prisoner who had been liberated. [EN-L:
Grandmothers of the Plaza de Mayo] Here, in part,
is what he had to say.

" . . . we were there, in La Cacha, chained and
abused, some of us wearing the blinding hood. But
there were a few remarkable prisoners who stood out
from the rest because of some special characteristic—
the generosity of their spirit.

"There was a young man who was called Raúl
whom I'll never forget because of his inner strength
and his capacity for empathizing with the other
prisoners. He had been several months in La Cacha
when they brought in a young kid in very bad shape.
I believe his name was Roberto. To my way of thinking
he was in serious psychological condition. He was
like a robot. He didn't talk, he didn't eat, he just
stayed in one place for hours and looked off at a fixed
point on the wall.

"Raúl immediately took the kid under his wing
and gave him all the care he possibly could. Seeing
the kid so emaciated, he began to give half of his food
ration to Roberto. This extra food, I became
convinced, is what kept the young kid from starving
to death. I realized then the tremendous force of
Raúl's will and his great sense of humanitarianism.
His attitude was "We are here in prison, but we can't
stop behaving like human beings. Precisely here,
where we are all equal and no one has anything, we
should not just be thinking of ourselves.

"Raúl took such good care of the kid that he
himself began to get thinner. But meanwhile Roberto

put on weight and became more animated, and even talked a little.

"One day the prison guards congratulated Raúl in a mocking way, suggesting he might win the Nobel Peace Prize. And then, when they saw Roberto in good spirits and fine health, they opened the cell door and announced: "Okay, kid, you're just fat enough now to be 'transferred'." And so they took Roberto away and we all supposed that they shot him." [EN-M: Euphemisms]

## "Kika"

One day a man came alone to see a group of us Mothers. He told us that he wanted to speak with just a few of us, to tell us what he knew very quickly and then be done with the whole business. He said that in a few days he would be on his way to Mexico with his wife. "I want to see if I can forget everything—to find out if I can begin again." So we arranged to meet with him later. We expected everything—and expected nothing. We would listen to his account the same as all those other stories we had heard from released prisoners who dared to find us and speak out.

In the beginning we just asked him the usual questions that, though it's hard to believe, had become a routine. "Where had he been arrested? When? How long had he been a prisoner?" And we would cross our arms and listen, our eyes riveted on him, hoping for some miracle.

He started by telling us that he had been taken from the detention center at Campo de Arana to the one at La Cacha. "Probably in 1978," he added, "but I can't be sure—once you're inside you lose all sense of time."

He gave us his name, said that he was a lawyer and that, ironically, a couple of times his own torturers had asked him for legal advice. He told us about the people he shared cells with in the clandestine camp. He named so many prisoners in telling us about Arana that we hardly had time to write them all down. But how in the world could we know if the Eduardo he spoke about was one of our sons? He said he was sorry not to be able to give us the full names of people he saw there, but, he said, "the truth is that during all that time I didn't even know my own name." He suggested that perhaps we could figure things out from his physical descriptions.

Then he began to talk about a boy who had been a prisoner for more than two years and another one at Arana whom he didn't know very well but who slept near him. "Whenever the jailers let him, the boy would come over to talk with me. All he did was talk about his little sister who was tall and dark—and a lot like his father." He mentioned that she must have been about 15. He also said that when he was born his father was hoping for a little girl, but that he had had to wait more than 10 years to have a daughter.

He said that he didn't know the young man's name, "but he was quite tall and very thin, like everyone who has spent more than a year as a prisoner. He always seemed to be deep in his own thoughts."

"Did he say he was a physics student or whether he was married?" I asked, feeling my heart jump out of my mouth at the prospect of having some news of Jorge.

"No, he didn't say. He only talked about his sister," the man answered, and he went on talking in the same vague way about other prisoners he had known.

Then he told us that, probably in March of 1979, he was moved to La Cacha with the promise that he would only spend a couple of months in that "rehabilitation institute". "That, of course, was a great irony," he commented. (Everyone knew by then that "rehabilitation" was just shorthand for "death").

Once in a while he had the chance to exchange a few words with some of the other prisoners. He immediately noticed "a kid, younger than me, who couldn't be more than twenty-five and always, despite everything that went on in the camp, seemed to be in good spirits. "One day he came over to me and asked me how I was and then quickly, because there was never much time to talk, he told me a little about his life. I was especially alerted when he spoke of a younger sister 'who looks a lot like me because we both take after my father'."

The other Mothers looked at me—was it possible that my sons were alive?

Then I burst in, "Try to remember, please. You have to remember! Did he tell you where and when he was detained, what his sister's name was? He must have said something."

"Please, let me finish," the man shouted at me. Then he continued. "Because of the way he described that girl, so close to fifteen years old, I immediately realized that he and that boy in Arana could be related. So I asked him, 'Don't you have a brother who is also detained?' 'Yes. Did you see him?' he asked."

"And then I told him that I had spoken with his brother in Arana and had realized they must be brothers because of their vivid description of their sister. For the next few months I had a number of short, interrupted conversations with him. In those detention centers someone asks something and the answer comes weeks later."

I had so many questions and so many urgent things spinning around in my head that I didn't say anything. But, I wondered, "How many pairs of brothers had been kidnapped and how many of them would have a little sister. Perhaps hundreds—there must be some sure way of knowing whether they were Jorge and Raúl."

I felt like crying and shouting all at the same time. I don't know if anyone is able to understand: my sons were still suffering, they were enduring torture and hunger, but in the midst of their horror, they had the good fortune to still be alive.

"You have to really try. Please. I beg you. Did he tell you if his name was Raúl? if his mother was called Hebe?"

"No. I believe he said his mother's name was Kika."

And then, finally, I began to cry, though not hysterically. I cried quite effortlessly and the tears just slid down my cheeks in silence.

## Raúl's Poem

As a postscript to her autobiography, Hebe wrote this account of Raúl's final communication with the outside world. It is the last report she was to receive from prison. It is troubling and puzzling—though hopeful, and even inspiring. For the reader it strikes a powerful, unresolved chord.

Every book of life is necessarily partial and leaves things out. And there are, I must now confess, things I have not even said to myself. This brief postscript is one of those that finally asks to be turned loose. It wants to be communicated even though for years it was a disturbing secret between Raúl and me and his intermediary.

That person was a young woman who had been pregnant when she got out of La Cacha, the same prison where Raúl was held. One day, long after she left there, for she had been threatened with death if she ever got anywhere near La Plata, she came to see me with an anonymity that was full of both modesty and mature understanding.

She didn't tell me very much about my son. She said that as her delivery date drew close she had been sure the authorities would take her out of the prison to have her child. Raúl then wrote on the edge of her skirt and told her my name and where I lived. "Don't read this now," he told her, because he didn't want to add sadness to her other burdens. "But if you should ever get back to the real world, give this piece of material to Mama. With a kiss." That was all Raúl said in the darkness of that cell. She made the promise.

When she visited me two years later she told me those things and then she held out the piece of gray, dirty cloth on which this poem was written. It was dated 1978 and was undoubtedly in Raúl's handwriting. He was speaking from a place that was beyond my knowing and I didn't have the heart to read it all. But still I couldn't resist it because it had too much intelligence and too much love in it. I have never been able to read it all until now, in these days of July 1985, when at times one feels that, truly, there is nothing left.

# "FERVENT PLEA TO A HOODED MOTHER"

by Raúl Alfredo Bonafini

I

You are all alone, Mama,
Alone with these three thoughts
whenever you think of me.
I, who am the future and prolonging
of your life,
I, who am in your womb,
speak to you, Mama.

I, who am growing with great strength
within your being,
I am the one who
will make your life happy.
Just wait patiently for my coming,
even though you are chained,
though you suffer and weep.

In your blackest, most sorrowful hours,
think about the future to come,
a future full of sunshine and greenness,
that we will share together,
very much together.

I, your son, am thinking all of this
as you, Mama, knit me a little sweater
and you worry and you cry . . .
and you are afraid.

I have a strange sensation now, Mamita.
It is something arising
from the many people nearby.
Arising from the affection of many chained bodies

who gaze at you as you walk by,
carrying me with you.
Their love and tenderness
make me grow stronger and healthier,
happier than ever, Mama.

## II

Now that I am about to be born,
I speak to you with the love of a child.
That love that you spread all around
is flourishing in me who is a part of you.
Don't be sad, Mama, for I am with you.
You are not alone.
I and hope are your companions
in your solitude.
That is the truth. Think about us.

The present time is hard for you,
but the inferno will pass
and everything will be again as it once was,
and even happier,
because I will be able to cry for you
so that you can cuddle me
and we can laugh together.

Everyone here wants to rock my cradle
They fill both of us
with the love I need
to be big and strong
when I come out from inside of you.

So, Mama, don't ever, ever forget
these thoughts of mine.
That way you will always have
the happiness that sustains me,
with infinite vigor,
within your being, Mama.

# CHAPTER 10

## THE MOTHERS GAIN CONFIDENCE
## AND A NEW MISSION

### A Turning Point

1980 was a kind of turning point for the Mothers of the Plaza de Mayo—suddenly a number of things began to go right. Our new office was a dream come true for us. For the first time we had a place to meet. No longer would we be wanderers who had to go secretly from church to church, from coffee shop to coffee shop, to have our meetings.

The office was on Uruguay Street, up some stairs and behind a glass door with a grille. All it needed was a little painting and polishing here and there. And it was ours, all ours. We had eleven sets of keys made. The night we got the office, I could hardly sleep. I was imagining hanging pictures, making curtains, bringing in plants.

We were all ecstatic as we entered our office for the first time. "Can you believe it, Juanita? All that we've been able to do in these past two years. We should do what Columbus did when he first stepped onto the New World." And I got down on my knees and kissed the floor. Dust never tasted any better! I didn't know whether to laugh or cry . . . .

Having an office made it possible for us to do more. Among other things, we began distributing a bulletin that told about the activities of the Mothers of the Plaza de Mayo. And now we had an address where we could get mail.

We soon began to receive invitations to go to Europe to speak at conferences concerning the human rights situation in Argentina. Of course our government learned about the invitations, but we didn't let this deter us. We accepted one of the invitations and decided that Nora de Cortinas and I would make the trip. It was an exhilarating time for all of us.

## Recognition and Awards

About this time a rumor began circulating that we might be candidates for the Nobel Peace Prize. Although the idea was exciting, it turned out that the award went to the Argentine human rights activist, Adolfo Pérez Esquivel. But as compensation, we soon received a call from Stockholm telling us that a check would be sent to the Mothers of the Plaza de Mayo so that two of the Mothers could go with the Argentine group accompanying Esquivel. Nora and I sat down with our calendars and figured out that our schedule of talks in Europe would make it possible for us to go to the Nobel ceremony. The Mothers' office was filled with euphoria. Humberto and Alejandra came in to Buenos Aires and other husbands and children joined us to share in this moment of high jubilation.

When the military heard that Esquivel had been awarded the Nobel Peace Prize they were enraged and called it a provocative act. In the beginning, the government was silent, but 24 hours later it announced that it was very surprised by the nomination of Esquivel and hastened to justify his year of arrest by alleging that his activities had been instrumental in helping various terrorist organizations.

Adolfo denied any such ties and reaffirmed his association with the Catholic Church. Esquivel declared that the true winners of the Nobel Peace Prize were the indigenous people of Latin America, the country people and the workers and all those who are fighting for human rights. He went on to say that it was imperative to reestablish real justice in Argentina for it is only justice that can help people find the path to peace.

The award ceremony in Oslo was moving. From the front row we all applauded Adolfo. The prize accomplished a double goal: it gave worldwide recognition to the importance of human rights and it was also a condemnation of the Argentine junta.

To our surprise, something else was waiting for us in Oslo—the news that the Mothers of the Plaza de Mayo were to be given an award of 157,000 Norwegian kronas, a lot of money, and an especially encouraging boost to our movement. We were thrilled by the prospect.

When Nora and I returned to Buenos Aires, after giving interviews with more or less half the population of Europe, we carried with us a pair of round trip tickets so that two of the Mothers could fly to receive the award. Maria Adela and Señora Epelbaum were the ones chosen to go. Our Mothers of the Plaza de Mayo was now beginning to reap some rewards after three long years of struggle on behalf of our disappeared children.

## A New Slogan

In 1980 we adopted our slogan **Appearance alive!**. Because when Adolfo Pérez Esquivel won the Nobel Prize, Emilio Mignone had gone with him and had traveled around Europe saying that the "disappeared" were dead. Not that we are naive or stupid, but we didn't want to give the dictatorship the chance to say that our children were dead when nobody had told us yet what had happened to them. And since no one had confirmed what had happened, we went on asking and demanding, and using that slogan—**Appearance alive!** This was just our way of keeping up the pressure and questioning the system.

## Renewed Repression

By the time we got back from Europe the junta had intensified the repression of the Mothers in the Plaza de Mayo. From the moment they realized that we seemed to be accomplishing something, we were punished. Every Thursday they would chase us, and would take two or three of us to the police station. They tried their best to humiliate and intimidate us.

Then and there we decided that if they took one prisoner we'd all go. So they took forty or sixty of us, not because they chose to, but because we made them take all of us prisoners. That's why some people said we were crazy. And if they didn't take us all, we went to the police chief on our own, and demanded, "Señor, I want to be a prisoner with all the other Mothers." The police chief didn't understand at all why we would want to be prisoners. There would be total confusion in the police station. There were no lawyers, no politicians to defend us. We were very much alone. Finally, usually toward dawn, they would release one Mother at a time. Other Mothers would be outside, marching around and protesting, until, at last, they let all the Mothers go.

The repression in the Plaza eventually became so brutal that we weren't able to go there anymore on Thursdays. We just went sporadically so we wouldn't lose the Plaza entirely. It was a matter of one Thursday in the morning and then a Friday afternoon. In the end things got so rough that we were forced to move our meeting place from church to church.

## March with Dutch Women

Early in 1980 we wrote to the women's' group in Holland inviting them to come to Argentina to see our new office. In March we had a telegram from them saying that yes, they would come and they would also bring reporters from Dutch television.

We were overwhelmed with good feeling; this would give us much more visibility with people in the outside world. They were listening to us and we were earning their respect. So why not make a party of it? We invited the ambassadors of Holland and Switzerland and their wives. Then we organized a march which would be led by a representative of the Dutch women's' group.

But the catch was that a state of siege was still in effect in Argentina and the authorities required us to check with them first because our march would involve international interests. Maria del Rosario and I went to see the appropriate military official.

"Do you know what this is?" the officer asked as he held up a piece of paper. "This is a decree. And do you know what it says? It says that during a stage of siege political acts or demonstrations are not permitted."

"All right," I answered. "Now let's see what else is prohibited."

"There's nothing more. That's all."

"Well, then, we can have our march because ours is 'a march of grief in silence'. And the decree doesn't prohibit . . . ."

The official sighed and gave in and there were no more arguments. We knew very well that he would get a calling down for his mute capitulation. He stammered that we were pulling the wool over his eyes. "When it comes right down to it, you women always get what you want."

Our march was powerful, beautiful. We walked in silence, as we had promised, and the long line of women was a wake-up call for anyone who still didn't believe what was going on in Argentina. One of the Dutch women led the procession and in Holland everyone saw us on television, marching together.

## The Mothers Retake the Plaza

For some time now, the junta's persecution of the Mothers had become so fierce that we hadn't been able to hold our Thursday processions in the Plaza de Mayo. But in 1980 we decided that we should retake the plaza, no matter what happened. And so we returned and started marching there again. We took the police by surprise because we went on a Thursday when they didn't expect us, at 3:30, our usual time. The next Thursday, at the same time, the police arrived ready for battle. They were up in the trees with their machine guns pointing down on us, watching us. But we stayed there anyway. They beat us, they turned their dogs on us, but still we said that we would keep going there. We felt that the Plaza had to be saved even though it was a struggle. It was a matter of the future; we felt strongly about restoring a constitutional government to Argentina, and living under the rule of law. We knew it was important to keep up our solemn processions of protest.

## Dealing with Threats

Some years later in a conversation with Alejandro Diago, Hebe accused the Argentine police and military of being so macho that they always underestimated the Mothers and thought of them as "poor little defenseless mothers", backward, or worse, as "those crazy women". [AD: 123-4] The military apparently never imagined that the Mothers could have such stubborn, wily ways. Nor did they ever dream that those poor, old "ignorant" women would have such a strong impact on Argentina.

My telephone was not tapped directly, rather it was a colander. There must have been ten little men inside it, all listening to our conversations. They didn't need to dial our number to threaten us; they were always there. "We're going to kill you" or "Tomorrow we will saw you into little pieces". After a while I took their words almost like a greeting, but in the beginning, when they were trying so hard to intimidate us, I was scared stiff.

At other times they would have all the lights in our house shut off. Then they would park their cars, filled with tough looking gangster types, in front of the house. They would stay there all night. Not only would our house be in total darkness, but the streetlights would be out too. The cigarettes hanging out of their mouths and the occasional flash of a cigarette lighter could distinguish my tormentors. They stayed there, out in the street—every night, smoking and spying on our house.

One time, during the raw winter of City Bell, they stationed four Ford Falcons at the corner. I made a bet with Toto—I put on a warm coat and ran out to their cars. They got out immediately.

"If you're going to spend all night keeping an eye on our house, may I offer you some coffee?" They didn't think it was the least bit funny and they didn't answer. They just started up their cars and raced off, tires screeching. Too bad—those characters never know what to do when someone is nice to them. In reality, they're just poor miserable souls who only know how to shoot a gun.

## Police Station

One fine day in 1981, our taxi pulled up to the offices of Monsignor Pio Laghi, the Papal Nuncio in Buenos Aires, where the flags of the Vatican and Argentina were flying over the entrance. Aurora and I had come to see this representative of the Pope, and we had brought files with information to back up our accusations about the dark side of the sainted Mother Church. We had complaints about the churches that had closed their doors to us, about the priests who had taken part in the repression, about the military chaplains who had been present during torture sessions, about those who had been informers in their parishes, and about those comfort-loving priests who had a file of the disappeared in their offices.

However, it appeared that the Papal Nuncio had changed his mind. He was no longer able to receive us. He said we should just leave our files. So, dejected, we left and walked along Avenida Alvear. Pretty soon it was clear that someone was following us. Within minutes, six policeman surrounded us.

"We need to do a background check, Señoras. You'll have to come with us to the police station. They'll have to do a computer check on you."

I just looked him straight in the eye and said, "We're not getting into your car."

The policeman seemed disconcerted. "Please, Señora, get in and don't make a scene," he stammered before grabbing me by the arm.

"Look, if you don't let me go immediately, I'm going to scream." Furious, the man let me go. "If you want us to go to the police station, we'll go in a taxi and you can follow behind."

The boss of the policeman lost face, but he called a taxi. His subordinate, quite disturbed by this official humiliation, gave me an angry look and told me that we'd have a good, long time to talk when we got to the station.

Once there I saw that it wasn't the federal police who were waiting for us but, instead, Army Intelligence. They controlled and supervised everything and took a dim view of the ordinary police. They put Aurora and me in separate rooms and took my briefcase away from me.

"Just a minute," I said. "Please make me an inventory of the contents now so there won't be any problems later."

They didn't seem to know what problems I was referring to. I tried to freshen their memories. "You don't know, eh? Well, for example, you might put in some pamphlets, or some damning papers or a book on subversive tactics—all those things you know how to do."

In my briefcase I had our accusations, copies of writs of habeas corpus and my personal amulets: photos of Sandro Pertini and Edward Kennedy. I always have the feeling that those photos protect me and make any aggressor pull back when they see that perhaps I have a little influence somewhere.

The police didn't know what to do with me and sent me to the Chief of Intelligence, a small, insignificant man, half bald, with gold-rimmed glasses. Maybe the most disagreeable man I've ever seen. He must have spent a long time practicing how to look like those Nazis in Hollywood movies. With his imitation of a German accent, he tells me that he will do my inventory and that he himself will conduct the interrogation.

"Good. But do the inventory in duplicate because I have a right to a copy too." The little Nazi refused to do it and was extremely irritated. He said he had no intention of making me a duplicate.

I could hear Aurora crying in the next room when one of the officers orders his men to bring in another of the Mothers who is making a scene in the reception room. She demands to see how we are being treated. "And if you don't let me, I'll start a rumpus in the newspapers." He lets her in.

"We're all right, Amanda. Just let our husbands know where we are." And then I turn to the officer: "Bring me the boss," I say, and I wink. As he turns to go, the duplicate slips its way into my pocket.

Then from Aurora's room I hear that little rat with the gold-rimmed glasses saying to Aurora, "You go to the Plaza because of that woman. She's a communist."

"No, Señor," Aurora's panicky voice answers. "I can assure you that I go because of my son."



They put me in a small room with a typewriter. The little man and his assistant arrive and the assistant sits down at the typewriter and the interrogation begins.

"What party do you work for?"

"None."

"Where do the Mothers get their money?"

"From international, charitable, and human rights organizations."

"International connections . . . ."

I look straight at him. I always look anyone in the eye who I consider trash.

The questions go on for three hours. They deride my "subversive sons" who they say work overseas. I tell them that they have been seen in the secret detention camps.

"Where do you get this business of 'secret detention camps'?"



"Bonafini!" a policeman suddenly shouts from the hall.

"Am I detained?" I shout back.

"No, it's just a background check."

"Then if I'm not detained, I'm Señora de Bonafini. If you don't use my proper name, I'm not moving from here."

"Bonafini! Bonafini!" he shouts again, louder and even more infuriated. They were going to treat me well or mistreat me, but I wasn't going to permit this arrogance on their part.

"Bonafini!" The shout grew in the hallway of the police station. I didn't move and I didn't answer.

Then, half an hour later, they called me once again: "Señora de Bonafini!" I heard him this time and I went out into the hall. An official led me to the police chief's office where the little man was waiting, surrounded by a few tough-looking characters. (Even though they bring in the whole battalion, I'm going to stick to my same answers because they're the truth.)

Finally the police photographer came in, a scraggly young man with a pock-marked face, a tiny rooster who brought an antiquated camera and a screen. He stood me in front of a white wall while two assistants held up the screen and then he began firing orders at me.

"Front view! Now profile!"

"That's enough, kid. Don't think you're going to keep me here for five hours with this screen!" The kid made a face and looked at the little man with the glasses who was enjoying it all and trying to suppress a laugh.

"Bring in the finger-printer right away," the Buenos Aires Nazi shouted and in a matter of minutes another policeman had covered my fingers with black powder and had pressed my fingers against a small piece of wood covered by paper. Once finished, he handed me a sliver of paper to clean my hands. "I need soap and water." The policeman then led me through corridors to the prisoners' bathroom. It was the pits: the smell of ammonia and stale urine made the air unbreathable, and the latrine was a hole spattered all over with shit. It must have been years since the place had been cleaned. I looked at my hands and I began to peel off the black paste of the fingerprinting powder and to smear it all over my arms up to my elbows. I came out holding my hands over my head.

The little Intelligence man took this opportunity to denigrate me for my gray hair. "Now you think you're some kind of grand lady, don't you." But eventually he backed down and took me to the bathroom that the police chief used and they gave me a clean towel and a piece of soap.

But you have to be on guard against the polite ways of military officials. Now they refused to let me have my briefcase back. I expect they were taking pictures of everything in it right down to old bus tickets.

Finally they let me go. It must have been two in the morning and Aurora had been waiting for me outside for hours. And there, in the street, totally dark except for the lighted door of the police station, was our Chevrolet and the silhouette of a man lying back in his seat. Who knows how many hours he had waited there with the radio tuned to tangos. He unlocked the door and smiled. Finally Humberto spoke.

"All right, now tell me. Did they interrogate you? Did they do anything to you?"

"No. What are they going to interrogate me about? They didn't lay a finger on me. They held us for six hours, mostly just sitting there and waiting."

Then I began to worry about the perverse way they could use those photos they had taken of me. Perhaps they would show them to Jorge and Raúl or to other prisoners who knew me, or to Azucena, to convince them that the Mothers' movement had been wiped out. Who knows what lies they might dream up.

I stopped thinking about all that as soon as we got home. Alejandrita had left a plate of food for me. The table was set for one, for me. I ran to her room and I woke her up with a kiss. Dinner was delicious. I felt curiously refreshed. The fight would go on.

## Resistance March and Fast

We had our first Resistance March in 1981—twenty-four hours of resisting the dictatorship in the Plaza. Some seventy or eighty Mothers stayed there, marching, all through the night.

Soon afterwards we took over the cathedral in Quilmes and a small group of Mothers fasted there for ten days. Both the Resistance March and the fasting demonstrated our desire for a constitutional government that would permit us to come out of that night of horrors with the hope—still—of finding some of the disappeared and, above all, of punishing those responsible. We already had a list of the military leaders whom we believed, naively, we were going to be able to both condemn and punish.

## New Directions

In 1982 the war in the Malvinas Islands (Falklands Islands) became another milestone for us. The Mothers declared their solidarity with the mothers of the soldiers who were fighting in the Malvinas. [See AR:465] But of course we opposed that war which is only another "red herring", like the World Cup, designed to divert the Argentines from other problems in the country such as the sad state of the economy and the continuing political dictatorship—and the disappeared.

People accused the Mothers of being unpatriotic and asked us how we could go to the Plaza while there was a war going on. This just prompted our placard **The Malvinas are Argentine, the disappeared also.** We remained firm in our stand and proclaimed that the justification for the war was a fabrication, an attempt to distract people from the dreadful situation on the mainland of Argentina. Once again we had to rely on the full realization of what had happened to our children to make us understand how tremendously criminal our military leaders were.

# CHAPTER 11

## THE END OF AN ERA

### Recovery

Slowly, and it was painful, I began to acknowledge the fact that persecution had become a part of my everyday life. But still, in spite of everything, I knew that as long as I lived I would never give up looking for our sons.

I didn't realize it at the time, but eventually I somehow began to laugh again—probably about something totally foolish. With that recovered smile there also grew a new gratitude for the people who had shared in all the difficult times with me—especially Toto. It was he, more than anyone, who tried to ease my sense of sadness. He was my companion through it all. Not until one night when we walked so tranquilly along the sidewalks of City Bell did I perceive all the importance of that word "companion". He took my hand, but it wasn't just his hand he was giving me. It was the profound love of his entire self. His love came to me across all those miserable years and all the misfortunes that we have shared. But his love also came to me across past happiness.

I worried now that, after everything that had happened, our future together had little chance of happiness. But

Humberto seemed to say that there were such times ahead of us, that I should just let myself rest on his shoulder and be confident that we would again have happy moments together. We had one another—now perhaps more than ever. And we still had Alejandra. Someday we would be grandparents!

"We have been a beautiful family," he said very softly as his eyes were lost on the tops of trees moving in the breeze. He was very certain that we had been a beautiful family.

Perhaps the most important thing I realize now is that we have not escaped the weight of history. We have accepted engagement with our time. We have taken up the burden. It is a little difficult to think about this in individual terms. It sounds grandiose—but it's real. We have been able to overcome our circumstances, the circumstances of our time in history.

## Toto's Death

Then, one day in 1982, the unexpected happened.

"I can't get up. I can't move . . . ."

"No, this can't be," I say as I sweep the house.

I had gotten up early to leave everything ready. Humberto was still in bed. "It must be fatigue or stress . . . ."

"I tell you, Kika, I can't move." I didn't mind that he shouted at me. What I did mind was that it was a shout of fear.

Later the doctor told me about the seriousness of Humberto's condition. It all sounded impossible—I wondered if there could be some mistake in the X-rays. The doctor rejected that suggestion.

Humberto had no idea how serious things were. We pretended it was pneumonia when in reality it was cancer that had metastasized. I had decided that they shouldn't operate if they couldn't save him. I only hoped that he wouldn't suffer, that he'd die in peace.

## The Mothers Intercede

The day I returned to the Mothers' office, Marta was there to meet me. "What are you going to do, Hebe?"

"What we all do—endure. We always say we wouldn't be able to take it, but when something like this happens, in the end we always come through."

The next time the Commission of Eleven met I asked to speak. "I could perhaps beat around the bush, but my conclusion is simple and direct. I resign from the Commission. I can't continue."

Right away the Mothers protested, their voices clamoring over one another. Maria del Rosario took my hand. Suddenly I needed to cry, so I left the room. While I was by myself I did some thinking. These Mothers weren't just my friends; they were my sisters. This group of women sustained me. To abandon them now would only heap pain upon pain. I went back to the meeting.

One of the most timid of the Mothers got up and smiled. Her voice was clear. "The Commission has decided that if it's all right with you, we'll all travel to City Bell. If you could ride the bus to Buenos Aires for all these years, it's only fair that we come to you now." She smiled from her heart and I began to cry.

Humberto weathered the winter fairly well, mostly by just sitting in a comfortable chair on the sun porch. Fortunately that remarkable man who had sustained the household during the disappearances of our sons was not able to see his own decline.

And yet the two of us knew that we were both pretending, that we were ignoring the inevitable. At times our eyes would meet and there would be a recognition of the absolute, undeniable truth.

I stopped going to the Plaza de Mayo for more than four months. Then one day my friend Gladys Ponti drove me to Buenos Aires in her car. As we rode along I was silent, anxious to get there. The memories of hundreds of Thursdays in the Plaza were multiplying in my head.

When I got there everything was as it should be, except that my heart was beating like a madman's. The Mothers with their kerchiefs, the young people who marched with them (more each time), some workers who had come directly from factories, several priests who never missed a Thursday and a few secretaries—a sad procession lasting for an hour. The hidden strength of this group was still there. I alone really understood how much I needed to march after all those months away. For me that weekly sharing had become a vital necessity.

On the way home I felt much better. At least, I thought, there is something that isn't going to change.

Humberto no longer knew what was going on. Gladys and Haydee often stayed with me through the night in the last weeks. There was always one of the Mothers there with me through those terrible, interminable nights when, despite being worn out, I couldn't sleep and I needed the gentle calm of their company.

At the end Humberto called for me all the time, but he neither saw nor heard me. He looked like a lunatic, he became violent and, finally, we had to take him to the hospital. Two days later, at one thirty in the morning on September 16, 1982, Humberto died.

## Reflections on Death

It was very hard to learn to live without Humberto's presence; not only in my heart, but also in all the little things I did every day. I was definitely alone, empty, without the person who had always been a good counterweight to my needs, the person who gave me my sense of identity.

It has always seemed to me a tremendous thing that one is capable of adjusting to the worst situations. Humberto's absence has now been transformed into a serene acceptance.

I began to think about death in a very personal way. I recognize all the guises of death; it has visited me too often in a very short time. But, curiously, all those deaths are but one single death and there is one single pain, great and persistent, that is always floating to one side of all my moments. It does not keep me from having deep happiness, or a good hearty laugh, or good humor. It knows how to stay to one side—but it never moves from there.

Death might graze me, but it would not phase me. (Ah— my old sense of omnipotence—if you could only read this, Humberto!) This is an obsession of mine and does not diminish with time. On the contrary. Every day it becomes more real. The junta is not going to be able to make me lie down and go quietly, and they know it.

## Strange Contentment

I am even happy sometimes when I think about my strong family and how fortunate I have been. I look back at Toto and myself as a young couple, with no worries, with our god of progress and well-being—and then I see the changes in our life and the way that, together, we have come to terms with our lives and have been able to overcome all those calamities.

From those first indiscreet meetings of adolescent eyes to that bed in the hospital, we have resisted all the storms together and that rather small link of our first love has now become a sturdy chain. Humberto is tangible and real, just as Jorge and Raúl are. They remain with me with a vigor that is very much alive.

I choose to stop here in the story of my life because, without doubt, Humberto's death marked a "before" and an "afterwards" for me. And yet, in one sense, this story has no end because my life and my work continue on and they are not going to be stopped. I am so sure of that! They are never going to be able to stop us. Not one hundred dictatorships, nor a hundred democracies, not a whole burst of machine-guns will be able to stop me. The reason for this is that I bear no weapons, only a closed fist where I keep the truth. That fist is not to beat anyone—it is for raising with a shout and opening the hand so that everyone can see the truth. And that hand will also be a sign that I demand what by law belongs to me—the confession and punishment of all those guilty of disappearing so many people in Argentina.

# Coda 1

## The Mothers As Seen in 1983

On the surface in 1983, the balance sheet for the Mothers of the Plaza de Mayo looked grim. For all their energy and courage and commitment, the Mothers did not get their children back. But despite this disheartening reality, their struggle accomplished something of enduring significance. They were eminently successful in confronting, head on, the silence and fear brought on by the all-encompassing repression of the military junta.

That silence came in many guises: the silence of the public out of ignorance and fear; the silence of the many people who were in sympathy with the junta—or worse, who cooperated with it; and, perhaps the most troublesome, the silence of denial with which so many in Argentina reacted to the stories of what was happening in their country. By leaving much of Argentina in a state of near paralysis, this pervasive silence tended to make the general public tacit accomplices of the military regime.

In April of 1977 when a small group of Mothers first dared to march openly in protest in front of government buildings in the main square of Buenos Aires, the silence imposed by the junta was publicly broken. As the marches became a weekly event, it was much harder for people not to be aware of the disappearances that were occurring with such frequency. This stepping out by the Mothers into the public eye and into the threatening world of police and rifles had a strong impact on their country. The Mothers' defiant, non-violent presence in the historic heart of Buenos Aires helped significantly to bolster the spirits of a terrorized populace and encouraged others not to be silent but to join them in marching in protest against the repression of the military regime.

Over time the Mothers also became exceptionally effective in helping to make the international community aware of what was really happening in Argentina. The Mothers successfully countered the junta's efforts to give the world the impression that life in Argentina was both happy and normal. With their white kerchiefs bearing the names of their disappeared children, the Mothers became a moving symbol of the tragic disappearances in Argentina and of the power of peaceful protest.

Because of their marches in Argentina and their international visibility, the Mothers contributed to bringing about the downfall of the dictatorship in 1983 and they deserve tremendous credit for having kept up the pressure on the military junta and for bearing witness to the criminal disappearances during the horrendous years of the Dirty War.

In the report of the Argentine Commission on the Disappeared, Ernesto Sábato singled out the importance that international concern for Argentina played during the days of the Dirty War. He gave the Mothers high praise, saying "the springboard for this mobilization of universal consciousness was the unsung, heroic achievement of the Mothers of the Plaza de Mayo . . . ." [NM: 426]

Not with guns, but with their feet, the Mothers demonstrated the resilience of the human spirit and the potential of non-violent protest to confront lies and deception with the truth. Just as Gandhi showed with his movement for Indian independence and just as the civil rights movement made clear in the United States, the Mothers exposed the myth that power necessarily depends on physical force. This is the legacy of the Mothers' formative years.

In 1983 many people idealized the Mothers as heroines. After the fall of the dictatorship, Hebe recalled that whenever the Mothers went to stadiums, plazas or theaters they would be greeted by a warm and emotional reception. [AD: 182] They had become known well beyond Argentina as champions of human rights and non-violent protest.

In 1983 these peaceful, determined middle-aged women were models for women's protest groups around the world. That image, however, has gradually eroded as the Mothers have continued to evolve in surprising, even shocking, ways over the next two decades.

# PART TWO

## THE EVOLUTION OF THE MOTHERS OF THE PLAZA DE MAYO AFTER 1983

The power of the dictatorship began to unravel in 1980. The economy was in a chaotic state and the Argentine people were extremely restless. Support for the military junta diminished even further after the military defeat of Argentina in the Falkland Islands War of 1982. Finally the deteriorating economic situation, plus widespread political unrest, combined with international pressure to bring about the collapse of the military junta. In 1983 the dictatorship was voted out by the democratic election of Raúl Alfonsín.

Almost from the very beginning of the Dirty War, the Mothers viewed the Argentine government as their enemy. Hebe said that the Mothers felt that they were "a direct product of the injustice of men, not just of the oppressors, but also of those who covered up for them. If the church had listened to us, if the judges had answered us about how to deal with the habeas corpus, and if the politicians we went to had not remained silent, we would not have gone to the Plaza." [AD: 123]

Over time, the Mothers' anti-government stance hardened and expanded until it included governments anywhere that they felt were oppressing people. It is these changes in the

Mothers' attitudes towards governments, as well as shifts in their images of themselves and in the causes they supported, that define the evolution of the Mothers of the Plaza de Mayo for the next twenty years.

# THE MOTHERS UNDER DEMOCRATIC GOVERNMENTS

## CHAPTER 12

## THE GOVERNMENT OF RAÚL ALFONSÍN

# (1983-1989)

### Frustration and Disillusionment

With the downfall of the dictatorship, the Mothers' movement might have come to a quiet, resigned end. Knowing that Alfonsín had campaigned on a human rights platform, they were at first optimistic. The disappearances and killings and torture were over, and Alfonsín, in his inaugural address, assured the Argentine people that "the atmosphere of public immorality" was a thing of the past. But profound differences between the government and the Mothers soon emerged. Instead of fading away, the Mothers group kept right on protesting and transforming itself with new goals.

One of the problems was that the Mothers' and Alfonsín's goals were somewhat at odds. Alfonsín's chief concern was to try to establish democracy and keep it stabilized. That implied, among other things, placating a military that was intent on preserving its power and not being held responsible for its acts during the Dirty War. Although the Mothers wanted a true democracy in Argentina, they had no sympathy with the military. Unlike Alfonsín, they did not feel that they had to weigh their own actions against the possibility of a military uprising. Their preoccupation was learning what had happened to their children and they remained adamant about the need to bring to trial and punish those in the military who were guilty of horrendous crimes.

Soon after Alfonsín took office, a delegation of the Mothers had a frustrating experience when they went to visit him.

He received us very well, very nice, very North American with his smile . . . . He gave us hope. A little later we had another interview with him and he told us that he believed that there were disappeared who were alive and what did we think. We told him we also thought that there were disappeared, still living. And do you know what he did by way of searching for them? He sent a radiogram to everyone in the Army asking them if they knew anything about the disappeared. And with all the effrontery that characterizes the Army, they told him that they didn't know anything. That's how he looked for our disappeared children who might still be alive.[HM: 28]

## Outright Opposition to the Government

The Mothers' early mistrust of Alfonsín grew until they completely lost confidence in the new democratic government. To their dismay, the Mothers noted that although Alfonsín had claimed that he supported human rights, he never came out publicly and marched with the Mothers. They felt that Alfonsín was siding with the military and that this had led him to advance "the theory of two devils". To the Mothers this theory was tantamount to saying that the repressive actions of the Armed Forces should be understood as a necessary reaction to the violence of political terrorists.

Once again the Mothers articulated their anti-government position with protest marches.

We marched with our first banner, a banner designed to vindicate the struggle of our children. We declared on this banner that these children had fought, with the Argentine people, for justice, for liberty, for dignity . . . . And we also marched with silhouettes and photographs of the disappeared . . . [HM: 28-29]

## CONADEP and Nunca Más

During the transition to democracy, the Argentine people had the choice of whether to forget the Dirty War, or even to deny that it had ever occurred, or instead to squarely face the things that had happened during those horrendous days. Some people chose denial, many others were quite content to get on with their lives and simply take a "let bygones be bygones" attitude. The Mothers from the start felt that the terrible days of the Dirty War should never be forgotten. To his credit, Alfonsín, during his first month in office, set up the Argentine National Commission of the Disappeared (CONADEP) to investigate and report on human rights abuses during the Dirty War.

But the Mothers were opposed to CONADEP. They said that they rejected it because it was not a commission that they themselves had chosen or that the people had asked for. Rather, they argued, it was a smoke-screen, a device that Alfonsín created merely to gain time. Indeed, they were suspicious of Alfonsín's intentions, afraid of a whitewash, and dismayed because Alfonsín had not given the Commission power to subpoena the military. The end result was that the Mothers did not cooperate with CONADEP in any way. They didn't give the Commission any of their materials—they sent them no information on Jorge or Raúl or others of their children who had disappeared. They refused to go on a march in support of CONADEP.

Despite the obvious handicap of not having the testimony of any military officers, CONADEP, under the leadership of the writer Ernesto Sábato, took extremely seriously its mandate to find out all it could about the circumstances surrounding the disappearances during the Dirty War. Their report, entitled *Nunca Más* (Never Again), was both disciplined and detailed. Among other things, it covered detention centers, methods of torture, and gave horrendous information on a wide range of the people who had been disappeared.

CONADEP's final report, a document of significant importance, was published in 1984 as a book. There was no mention of it in the Mothers' official history.

## Trial of Military in 1985

A high point of Alfonsín's term as president was the trial in 1985 of nine top level commanders of the armed forces who were accused of crimes against humanity during the Dirty War. Before testimony was given, but anticipating that the trials would produce little to rectify anything, the Mothers marched in protest through the streets of Buenos Aires.

When the trial began, the Mothers were present in the courtroom every day as observers. Not surprisingly, Hebe was suspicious of trials that were held under the Code of Military Justice in civil courts—and without having the accused present in the defendant's box. Further, she criticized the trials because she alleged there was a tremendous amount of information that never came out in the trials. The only example she offered was that there was no mention of the complicity of multi-national corporations.

While Hebe had broad complaints about the trials, she chose to be confrontational in small matters as well. During the trial she found herself in conflict with the authorities about wearing the identifying kerchief of the Mothers of the Plaza de Mayo.

> . . . I had a long discussion with Julius Caesar Strassera [the lead prosecutor at the trial] about my kerchief. The authorities said I couldn't wear it in the courtroom . . . . Later, I took it out and put it on; Strassera came back and made me take it off again. But since I had a number of kerchiefs tucked away in my skirt, the authorities would take one away and I would pull out another . . . . Finally I said to Strassera "All these people here are wearing hats. Why don't you make them take them off? The police are wearing caps. No, for you the problem is the white kerchief. Dr. Strassera, the kerchief will end up being the only thing that is condemned in this trial." [HM: 33-34]

While the trial was being held there was a sudden rise of violence in Argentina—a series of bombings, and the threat of more violence, said to be the work of right-wing terrorists who were trying to force the government to give amnesty to former military leaders. To combat these threats, Alfonsín imposed a 60-day state of siege. Once again, the Mothers sensed the complicity of the military with the government. The trials continued until December. In the end, five of the nine military officers on trial were convicted; the other four were acquitted.

> When they announced the first acquittal, I got up and left the trial. What I regret is that I went alone because not one of my companions from the other organizations left too. I walked out all by myself but I was followed by many journalists who asked me why I was going. I told them that I had left because it was all a sham, because, by absolving assassins, they were thumbing their noses at the Argentine people and the people of the whole world. [HM: 34]

After the news of the acquittals of the military, a small group of the Mothers made an appointment to protest to Alfonsín. They arrived at the Government House at the scheduled time, but they found that the President had left for the day. But, staying on target, the Mothers decided to spend the night there and wait for Alfonsín; they had come prepared with pillows and blankets, tea and coffee. With journalists to witness everything they did, the Mothers took over the Government House for 20 hours in what they proclaimed was a successful political protest using neither force nor violence. Although they did not succeed in meeting with Alfonsín, the Mothers felt that they had shown what a determined group of older women could do in defiance of their government. They had now become full-fledged political activists energized by their anger and frustration.

## Still No Solution for the Mothers

Once the trials were over, Alfonsín, the military and a great many people throughout Argentina wanted to close the books on the Dirty War. The Mothers were strongly opposed to this position. They were afraid that they would never find out what had happened to their children, that the perpetrators of crimes against humanity would go unpunished and that all their efforts would have been to no effect. At this time the Mother's opposition to closing the books became a driving force in their lives. They stood their ground and fought to keep alive the memories of their children and the Dirty War.

For the Mothers under Alfonsín's government, nothing had been resolved, little had changed. They still felt abandoned by the Catholic Church, they felt betrayed by the legal system; they were still vehemently opposed to the military. They mistrusted the new democratic regime, and, indeed, they were as fully opposed to Alfonsín's government as they had been to the junta during the days of the Dirty War. In short, the Mothers remained confrontational and once again became sharp thorns in the sides of the established government.

Everything they did from then on was based on their conviction that the proper course for them was to keep fighting. Week after week, and year after year, they marched and demonstrated, denounced and protested. They pressed for a list of those who had been implicated in the disappearances. They demanded confessions and civil trials of the military. **Prison for those who committed genocide!** their banners cried out. They openly targeted the military that still walked freely along the boulevards of Buenos Aires with shouts of **Assassins, Torturers and Gross sons of bitches.**

By such defiant actions, the Mothers kept alive the memory of the disappeared and warned the government that they would not be quiet, that they would not conform and that they would not let the government rest.

## Changes in the Mothers

Over time the Mothers began to form a new image of themselves. It was no longer enough just to go to the Plaza once in a while or to have a child who had disappeared; a Mother had to have an active militancy.

By 1979 the Mothers had come to the painful realization that their children could no longer be considered politically innocent, that they had not only been militant, but that they were also revolutionary activists. [AD: 211-212] Hebe confessed that she herself had changed too.

It was the disappearance of my sons that put me consciously on the left. But it took quite a while before I could acknowledge myself as a revolutionary militant. First I sensed it. Then I actually dared to say it. From 1980 on I began to feel that I should commit myself more and more to what I was saying. It was then, on a form from Switzerland where they asked me a great many pointed questions, that I began to make some more daring statements, starting with the recognition that our sons had been involved in something . . . . Already in 1979, or perhaps at the end of 1978, I had begun to realize that our children were taken away because of that.

I always remember a day when the Mothers were taking out an ad where we said that there were political reasons for the kidnappings; four mothers came to me then and said that they couldn't go along with the "ad" because their children hadn't done anything. "Ah", I said to them, "but then you can't be part of the Mothers of the Plaza de Mayo. You will have to join the mothers whose children were taken away because they were stupid." This was during 1979. [AD: 211-212]

Gradually Hebe became able to articulate her new political orientation: "Everything that concerns the fight for a new kind of man, for liberation, for total change and revolution, if it is Marxist, or communist, Maoist, Trotskyist, anarchist—even if is it all those "ists" together—if it synthesizes everything I want, well then that's what I am. It doesn't frighten me one bit, because I am already completely fed up with all the niceties of definition." [AD: 224]

As a corollary to this radical political approach, Hebe, like Che Guevara, advocated revolution as a way to effect significant changes in Argentina. She said that, as Argentines, "we have to accustom ourselves to thinking about revolution in our own country, with all the consequences." [AD: 213]

Hebe also picked up on a political theory of David Viñas, the Argentine writer and cultural critic, and espoused it as her own. She stated that the disappeared were like the Indians of Argentina who had been wiped out in the

19th century. In Hebe's words the argument was that Argentina, being a refined country, had perfected the means of getting rid of people who got in its way. The Indians, ("barbarians") of the 19th century, were exterminated by conquering their land, just as the revolutionaries ("terrorists") of the 1970's were made to disappear. "Thus," Hebe pronounced, "genocide has been perfected by means of disappearances." [AD:213]

On such a revolutionary trajectory, it was perhaps inevitable that the Mothers' definition of violence would change.

Violence begins with the pornography of showing you a plate of food that you aren't able to buy. Violence occurs when people work but aren't paid, or when you can't afford to enroll your child in a school—or when you get to the hospital and your child dies because he is malnourished. Or when workers have unsafe working conditions. For me the worst of all violence happens when a child dies of hunger. [AD: 206]

Is the people's reciprocal violence justifiable? I believe it is even more justifiable. The revolutionary guerrilla is part of an army of people that takes to the streets to find bread for their children and in that measure I justify violence and I condone it. [AD: 207]

## The Mothers Reject the Amnesty Laws

From the beginning of his presidency, Alfonsín was extremely apprehensive about an increasingly restive military. He understood fully the possibility of a coup. Apparently feeling that he had to be particularly circumspect in how he handled the military, Alfonsín responded by enacting two amnesty laws. The first, the Law of Due Obedience, enacted in 1984, proclaimed that lower-ranking officers should be allowed to absolve themselves by claiming that they had only been following orders and therefore should not be held responsible for their actions. The other amnesty law, the Final Point Law, was enacted in 1986 and set February 23, 1987 as the last date for any trials connected with the Dirty War. With these two laws, vast numbers of the military were virtually pardoned and it now seemed impossible to ever bring them to justice.

The Mothers, outraged by these events, denounced the complicity of the government and the military. The Mothers' official history also rejected the concept of collective guilt that, they said, the government implied by stating "we are all responsible, we are all guilty". The Mothers were unwilling to subscribe to the theory that all sectors of Argentine society had allowed the Dirty War to happen and that, for this reason, the military should not be the only ones to be penalized. Instead the Mothers accused the government of perpetrating the Dirty War. They argued that government authorities had enacted the amnesty laws because they were afraid, . . ."because they wanted to pardon themselves for all their crimes during the Dirty War. They are not just pardoning the military, they are also pardoning themselves." [HM: 38]

## The Mothers Object to Closure

The Mothers' rejection of the amnesty laws was predictable. To publicly register their opposition to the Final Point Law, they held a protest march, "The March of the Kerchiefs", that ended with a battle cry, **The military are all criminals.**

Indeed, they were objecting not merely to a particular law, but to all efforts to close the books. Such efforts began during Alfonsín's first month in office when he sent telegrams to the Mothers saying that their children were dead in such and such cemetery and sent some of them boxes with human remains that he asserted were their children.

This led the Mothers to begin deliberating about how they should deal with the whole matter of exhumations. They reasoned that if they accepted the exhumations of those killed in what authorities described as "confrontations", they would be accepting those deaths without anyone having told them who had killed their children, who had kidnapped them, without anyone telling them anything. They argued that it would encourage the military to go right on being assassins. The Mothers were the only organization that rejected those exhumations that for them had become another "final point". [EN—N: Exhumations]

So deeply felt was the Mothers' opposition to the exhumations of their children's remains that Hebe tried to prevent authorities and a forensic scientist from opening some of the first graves. As Bouvard recounts, when a judge attempted to prohibit her interference, Hebe said, 'If you touch one of those corpses, I am going to throw you in the grave head first". As a result, she was almost sent to prison. But, undaunted, Hebe confronted the judge, demanding to know what he had been doing all of those years when he was supposed to be investigating what happened to their children And, further, why he wasn't trying to find out who had ordered their burial. The unearthing did not take place. [MB: 149-150]

When the government proposed that reparations be paid to each mother as compensation for the loss of her child (or children), the Mothers firmly rejected such an offer— not just because they said that no amount of money could ever take the place of a missing child, but because, by accepting the government's money, the Mothers would be demonstrating their willingness to close the books on the past.

The Mothers also opposed use of commemorative plaques for their children. Their rationale was that there was the same sense of finality in those little plaques in some schools saying, "here so-and so studied" or "here so-

and-so worked". They rejected that kind of posthumous honor because they felt that it was yet another "final point". They said that the only way to honor their children was for the living to keep on fighting—just as the disappeared had fought. This became the guiding principle for the Mothers in all their actions.

## Negative Views of the Mothers

The Mothers already had a bad reputation with the government, the military establishment, and the church. Now many others also began to see them as a disruptive undercurrent that kept the country on edge. People wondered if the Mothers hadn't gone too far, if all their actions were fruitless and served only to fester the wounds of the Dirty War.

Disregarding signs of this disapproval, the Mothers continued to use strong stands and strong language, as well as dogged persistence, to confront the existing Argentine government. Such outright combativeness made many people look at the Mothers in a decidedly negative light. Some people saw them as "crazy", as "The Mad Women of the Plaza", as the mothers of terrorists, as too aggressive, as women who simply weren't able to come to terms with the loss of their children—and as a constant reminder of Argentina's painful past.

There loomed a decided fork in the Mothers' path. They had to decide if they wanted to keep challenging authority and refusing to cooperate with Alfonsín's government, or if they wanted to follow a more temperate path. Although the Mothers chose to remain confrontational, not all of its members agreed. In 1986 twelve of the women within the Mothers of the Plaza de Mayo who preferred to follow a more conciliatory, less radical path, broke off from the Mothers and started their own group named the Mothers of the Plaza de Mayo Founding Line, known more simply as The Founding Line.

Marguerite Bouvard, makes this observation about the split in the Mothers' group: "Class distinctions and education, as well as organizational models and attitudes towards the political process, distinguish the Mothers of the Founding Line from the Mothers of the Plaza de Mayo. The former are closer to the socio-economic and educational backgrounds of many feminists, among whom the split has aroused much controversy. Prominent scholars in both the United States and Argentina have supported the Founding Line, criticizing the Mothers of the Plaza de Mayo for their political style." [MB: 16]

There is no mention of this split in the Mothers' official history!

## The Front for Human Rights

The Mothers received a real injection of hope for their future in the mid 1980's when a group of young people came to them and offered to help them with the work of their movement. The Mothers had always wanted to remain autonomous and were generally cautious about accepting support from outside of their own close-knit organization. This time, however, they put aside their usual caution and welcomed the energetic help of the young people of the Front for Human Rights, a group that had been organized in 1985 to lend support to human rights organizations in Argentina. [MB: 197]

The Mothers spoke of them as their new children; they cooked for them and worried about their problems and said that they were as dependent on them as they used to be on their children. The young people, for their part, helped with the office work, making banners, producing flyers and joining the Mothers in marches and demonstrations. Hebe described it as a "beautiful relationship" that sprang up spontaneously and grew with time. She said that there was both love and humor between the two groups. [AD:187]

Thinking ahead to the future, Hebe told Alejandro Diago that the Mothers felt that they were laying the groundwork for the planting of a crop—planting the seed and watering it (as if with the blood of their own children), although the actual harvesting would be for others who would also be their children.

We are teaching the new children a little about the importance of political participation, about confronting the enemy and about calling things by their name: the assassin, the assassin, the repressor, the repressor. We are inflaming their hearts and awakening their consciences. [AD: 168]

What Hebe apparently did not realize at that moment was that those young hearts were already inflamed; their consciences had already been awakened. Indeed, they were on a more radical path than the Mothers. When Bouvard was in Argentina in 1990, she interviewed eleven members of the Front for Human Rights. They told her that "they had joined the Mothers' movement because of its revolutionary potential and that they supported the Cuban model, all the while insisting upon their lack of political affiliation". [MB: 197] Once again, as with Astiz, and again with serious implications, the Mothers had been infiltrated.

Through the efforts of the Front for Human Rights, the Mothers were invited to take part in the International Congress of Women in Cuba in 1988. Hebe led the Mothers group; they were there from September 28 to October 8, 1988. [AD: 144] While she was in Cuba, no doubt Hebe heard more about Che Guevera, whom Fidel Castro had eulogized in this way after his death on October 9, 1967: "If we want the.model of a human being who does not belong to our time but to the future, I say from the depths of my heart that such a model, without a single stain on his conduct, without a single stain on his behavior, is Che! If we wish to express what we want our children to be, we must say from our very hearts as ardent revolutionaries: we want them to be like Che!" [JLA: 741]

The Mothers became closely associated with anarchism and in June of 1990 adopted an anarchist platform. [MB: 228]

## Reactions to Military Uprisings

The military continued to be restless. The reality of their threatening presence made Alfonsín's government extremely nervous in 1988. When there was an uprising of the military, the Mothers denounced what they saw as the complicity of the government and the military. They registered their protest by marching and chanting the phrase they so often used: **The military are all criminals**.

There have been a number of reinforcing events in the Mothers' evolution. One of them can be identified by the words "La Tablada", an event directly connected with the continuing threats of a military that was intent on preserving its power and insuring its immunity for past actions. In 1989 when militant leftists, who were opposed to the military, tried to take over La Tablada barracks, confused reports indicated that the group had been brutally repressed by government forces. Politicians and human rights organizations were alarmed and began investigations. The Mothers publicly accused the government of the things that the few survivors of La Tablada had told them: that young people who had been surrendering with white flags were shot down, that once again people had been "disappeared", and that once again the government and the military had been accomplices. From then on, the Mothers spoke of "La Tablada" as a terrible episode and declared that it was the final internment of all democracy in Argentina.

Alfonsín's response to this tense situation was to tighten government control by creating a Security Council and drawing up an anti-terrorist law. The Mothers firmly repudiated these actions, which they saw as the government's way of repressing the people who were beginning to rebel against the desperate economic crisis in Argentina. The Mothers cited the connection between the tightening of security and the looting of supermarkets. They claimed that government forces had ferociously attacked the looters who were both unarmed and hungry. On March 24, 1989, the twelfth anniversary of the coup, Alfonsín declared a state of siege. The Mothers, in response, again declared that democracy was dead in Argentina.

Alfonsín's government was being overcome by economic forces and was falling apart. Indeed, the situation was so critical that Carlos Saul Menem, who had just been elected president of Argentina, took office six months early, on July 8th, instead of the usual inauguration day of December 10th.

# CHAPTER 13

## THE GOVERNMENT OF CARLOS MENEM
## (1989-1999)

### Undeclared War

The undeclared war between the Argentine government and the Mothers of the Plaza de Mayo continued, and even intensified, under President Menem. When the new government came in, the Mothers, as they had done with Alfonsín, asked for an interview with the president. An interview was never granted. Many people had high hopes for Menem's government—but the Mothers' organization was not among them.

From the beginning the Mothers felt that however much Menem tried to differentiate his administration from the previous regime, the outlines of his politics were the same and he would only accentuate them. "Immunity for the military and hunger go hand in hand", the Mothers observed. They were disheartened when, early in his presidency, Menem, hoping to bring unity and reconciliation to Argentina, urged the people to forget the past. His attitude was that the past had nothing more to teach the Argentine people.

Then there began to be talk of pardons for the few military who had actually been convicted. This would be the ultimate step the military needed to insure immunity for everything they had done during the Dirty War. In anticipation of these pardons, the Mothers demonstrated their strong opposition in a series of marches with the rallying cry, **We will not forget, we will not pardon**.

In February of 1990, when Menem's pardons were issued, an estimated 80,000 people marched in the streets of Buenos Aires in protest. To the Mothers the Dirty War seemed to have been given legitimacy. The Mothers now recognized Menem's ability to repress anything that was in opposition to his government. They assumed there was no longer any hope of prosecuting the military on human rights charges. Nevertheless, they protested and then they went to Europe where they vigorously denounced the pardons in press conferences and TV interviews. They even went before the European Parliament to denounce what to them was this latest attempt to obliterate the past. This was one of the Mothers' last sustained efforts to focus on the disappearances of their children.

## Evolving Causes

Although the Mothers remained faithful to their earliest goals of finding out what had happened to their children and prosecuting the guilty military, they evolved in important new ways, especially in the kinds of causes they chose to support.

Key to the Mothers' gradual transformation was their emphasis on the ideals of truth and social justice that they felt had inspired their children. They spoke of their sons and daughters as militants who had given their lives for a utopia and they identified their children as the ones who had given birth to their own beliefs and actions—indeed, to everything that the Mothers had become.

As the Mothers expanded their goals, they tried to persuade people in Argentina to follow the path of liberation and social justice that their children had marked for them. But to do this the Mothers became convinced that it was tremendously important to organize the people, barrio by barrio, so that they could work collectively. There is now an urgent, mobilizing tone as the Mothers write their history.

As long as we live, we will go on struggling for the life of the Argentine people, a people who now appear to be tired, defeated and depressed, but who, when they are called upon, will rise up and take to the streets. But they will have to be organized . . . so that someday we will have a government that will really represent the people . . . a government that with justice will condemn the assassins who made us live through so many atrocities. [HM: 42]

At a time when people were protesting against Menem's severe economic policies, the Mothers gave their wholehearted support to the workers. The Plaza, they felt, now also belonged to the workers; it had become a space dedicated to resisting oppression, a place where the workers' struggle joined the struggle of their disappeared children.

With the firmness of their convictions, the Mothers stood behind the workers in a variety of ways. They supported a forty-five day railroad strike and a hunger strike, they let strikers and protesters use their house, their telephone, their fax machine and their contacts.

The Mothers then went on to support the student movement that opposed the government's law limiting access to education. In reaction to this challenge from the students, Menem made a bone-chilling threat: he warned the parents of the students that if those young people didn't stop demonstrating, if they didn't stop marching, fighting, and denouncing, there would be many more Mothers of the Plaza de Mayo in Argentina. [AR: 555]

Undaunted, the Mothers later took up the cause of the 5000 prisoners who were protesting against the miserable conditions in Argentine prisons. Although the Mothers' actions made the public more aware of this problem, the group had no illusions about their chance of achieving any radical improvements. Their eyes were fully open to what they saw as the basic cause of the problem: prisons were not to serve justice but to repress the opposition of people living on the margins of society. "Not one of the people who afflicts the Argentine people will go to prison. Our prisons serve a purpose, depending on what class a person comes from. That is how they keep our system alive." [HM: 59]

In August of 1990 when Menem was sounding out the possibility of imposing the death penalty, the Mothers again opposed him. They argued against the death penalty and pointed out that it was practiced every day in Argentina, and not just by trigger-happy police who decimated the poor barrios. The Mothers claimed that the death penalty was given to thousands of people through unemployment and through the hunger that, they said, caused the death of one child every twenty minutes in greater Buenos Aires. The Mothers even alleged that death itself lay at the massive base of a governmental system that made every dissenter disappear.

## Protests and Reprisals

President Menem was extremely uncomfortable with the Mothers' public denunciations and demonstrations and would clearly have liked to drown out their cries for justice. Severe reprisals against the Mothers for taking up causes opposed by the Argentine government were soon to occur.

In April 1990, a "Hero Commander of La Tablada" sent Hebe a telegram saying that she had been condemned to death and that she would be executed when they found her. This was the first of a series of intimidations and attempts on her life that lasted all year and that reached its most dangerous when a car tried to run her over on the sidewalk. Hebe escaped unhurt. After that, the Mothers sensed that their strong ties of solidarity with the outside world put some restraint on these attacks.

By this time the Mothers were being given little coverage in the media, the lights were turned off in the Plaza when they went there to march in the evening and the number of people who dared to march with them noticeably decreased. With threats and reprisals, actions and reactions, the battle between the Mothers and Menem continued. One of the Mothers' boldest actions in 1990 was on the 9th of July (Argentina's Independence Day) in front of the Cathedral in Buenos Aires where the government was holding the Te Deum before a military parade. The Mothers suddenly appeared at the door of the Cathedral and to everything the Cardinal said they answered in unison, **Thou shall not kill, thou shall not rape, thou shall not steal** and they each held up the photo of a disappeared person. Then, as the dignitaries were leaving the mass, the Mothers shouted at them, one by one, as they passed by, **Neither forget nor forgive, one hundred years of prison**.

In 1991 there were four attacks in forty-five days on the Mothers' house. Armed forces entered at night, destroying everything of significance in the house.

They stole things that were of great sentimental value to us—or that were fundamental to our history (like the rosary the Pope gave us, the sword that had been presented to us by people in Colombia, the medals won by the young men who fought in the Malvinas War, and all the photographs of the police that we had in our archives). We believe that that was the real object of these attacks because, at bottom, despite their violence and brutal strength, they are cowards and they are afraid of us. [HM: 53]

Two years later, when Menem held a constitutional convention to try to change the Argentine constitution so that he could run for president again, a delegation of Mothers traveled to Paraná and vehemently opposed this plan. At the Te Deum in the cathedral there, as authority figures at the church service passed by, the Mothers once again bombarded the clergy, politicians and military with their shouts and chants of recrimination.

## Additional Radical Causes

In the early 1990's, the Mothers of the Plaza de Mayo were known for their peaceful protest and were a positive force in various parts of the world. They had international support, especially from Spain and Holland, where streets and plazas were named for them. They were given awards and honored for their non-violent struggle. Women's organizations and human rights groups around the world invited them to conferences. Journalists, jurists, and representatives of human rights organizations visited the Mothers' house in Buenos Aires—as did activists such as Pete Seeger and Jane Fonda.

In this new stage of their evolution, the Mothers traveled abroad to universities and conferences, giving speeches and meeting with like-minded groups from many different countries. Representatives of the Mothers went to France, Holland, Belgium, Germany, Spain, North Korea, the Philippines and the United States. And always they talked about the disappeared in Argentina. Hebe said that the thing that made them happiest was that everywhere they went "we find men and women who really want to know our story. They themselves are victims who are rebelling and resisting and they think of us as their models or mentors." [HM: 55]

The Mothers' extensive travels and their exposure to a wider world of ideas and problems were important steps in their gradual transformation. No longer were they just concerned with their own children or the actions of the Argentine government; they began to use their considerable energy on behalf of different sets of victims in other parts of the world.

Over the years the Mothers had naturally been sympathetic with the concerns and complaints of indigenous people; it was to them that the Mothers' activism now shifted. As October 12, 1992 approached, the Mothers referred to it not as the 500th anniversary of the day that Columbus discovered America, but as "the beginning of the first genocide, the beginning of a long submission, of a long period of blood-letting on our continent." [HM: 55]

The Mothers celebrated "Columbus Day" by presiding at an Alternative Summit in Madrid. Later they participated in a people's forum on Emancipation and American Identity at which there was an unveiling of a monument to commemorate the victims of genocide in Latin America. This experience led the Mothers to declare "the millions of assassinated, indigenous people, the thousands in Latin Americans who have died fighting for freedom, have become our brothers in spirit and are with us always." [HM: 55-56]

In 1994, when the indigenous people of the state of Chiapas in Mexico rose up in armed rebellion, the Mothers gave them their enthusiastic support. They sent letters of solidarity, they protested at the Mexican embassy demanding that the oppression be stopped, they denounced the presence of the Argentine military among the forces trying to put down the rebellion.

The Mothers considered that an especially significant event in their evolution was a meeting, in 1994, of women from around the world who had been supportive of them. This meeting gave the Mothers a new focus and instilled their work with a sense of solidarity with women from diverse parts of the globe.

For the three days of this meeting, The Mothers Who Fight talked freely among themselves, behind closed doors. We were mothers of the disappeared from several Latin American countries, from the Sahara region, mothers of children in the Ukraine who are victims of terrible ecological crimes, women who have joined together against the Mafia in Italy, and against fascism in Israel, women who are trying to help the victims of the war in Yugoslavia, and of the repression in Palestine, Spanish mothers who want to support their children in not joining the armed forces, or who have banded together to save their children from the inferno of drugs . . . .

Of course these women represent very different lives and have very different stories to tell, but as we began to hear their testimonies, we noted that there was a common denominator: death. At that moment we realized that our struggle in Argentina was part of the same struggle: the fight for life. [HM: 57-58]

## Opposition to the United States, the United Nations and Imperialism

The Mothers' efforts on behalf of victims in various parts of the world encouraged them to denounce imperialism and organizations that, they believed, supported it. The first such occurrence came in 1994 when the Mothers went to the United Nations International Congress on Human Rights in Vienna. It was not in a supportive role.

. . . the United Nations is an organization with which we have had many differences from the very first day. We were especially disturbed when they told us that Jimmy Carter would give the inaugural address. We, who knew very well the attitude of the United States during the dictatorship, began to chant **Carter, No!, Carter, No!** and then to shout so loudly that it kept him from beginning his speech. When the journalists asked us what all the shouting was about, we told them that they were the cries of all the people who had ever been tortured and killed by the sinister hand of imperialism. Alternative forums and street demonstrations became the most important happenings at that United Nations assembly which for a long time has been condemned to serve the paralyzing strategy of the oppressors. [HM: 56]

Strong expressions of anti-American feeling begin to run through Hebe's written and spoken words. According to Alejandro Diago's interview with her, Hebe's hatred for the United States was generated by her conviction that U.S. arms were "behind the subjugation of our people" and that the Argentine military were "educated like robots in the military doctrine of the U.S.". [AD: 138, 215] Hebe stated that she believed that the average North American is a cold, calculating person who looks out for himself and doesn't worry about who gets killed. [AD: 139]

## Disillusionment with Democracy

Back in Argentina, in 1995, Hebe gave a speech that clearly demonstrated her thorough disillusionment with democracy and the Argentine politicians. She mentioned that elections were coming up but that many Mothers were not going to vote because they felt that it wouldn't change anything.

For the Mothers, Hebe said, democracy is just a fiction where the people are encouraged to believe that they are deciding their destiny, while, in reality, everything is resolved in secret. Hebe accused Argentina's leaders of being corrupt puppets who just replace one another. In her view, it is the developers, the financiers, the bankers, and the multinational entrepreneurs who actually pull the strings.

## Taking Advantage of the Scilingo Affair

From 1983 until a thoroughly disturbing revelation in 1995, a great many of the Argentine people had somehow been able to ignore or suppress the unnerving events of the Dirty War. Although *Nunca Más*, the CONADEP report, had been available to a wide public in 1984, perhaps it was too much to expect that a people who wanted to return to a normal routine would be willing or able to assimilate so many horrifying facts. Even the trial of the military in 1985 did not seem to be enough to awaken thoroughly the country to its frightening recent history. Part of the blame for this burying of the past lay in a deliberate attempt to obscure what had happened during the Dirty War with an official order "to burn all documentation" given to the armed forces just before the downfall of the junta. After that, a screen of secrecy continued to shield those who had played such a devastating role in the Dirty War. The military carefully cultivated this pact of silence that made it impossible for the Argentine people to take the full measure of what had really happened during the dictatorship of 1976-1983.

This official silence was finally broken on March 2, 1995 when *El Vuelo* (The Flight) by Horacio Verbitsky hit the bookstores and the public learned, in shocking detail, about the systematic flights that carried more than 1500 people to their ocean deaths. The revelations made by Verbitsky, one of Argentina's most respected journalists, were based on the transcribed confessions voluntarily given to him by Adolfo Francisco Scilingo, a man who had played a key, and incriminating, role in two of the flights. It was his haunting memory of having personally hurled prisoners to their deaths that had impelled him to confess to Verbitsky.

Even after so many years, Scilingo's sensational, almost believable, account of regular Wednesday death flights from The Naval Mechanics School immediately became a nightmare for Argentina. The pain of the past was not only there for all to see in the pages of Verbitsky's book; it was now unmistakably present on radio and television in recorded tapes of Scilingo's conversations with Verbitsky. "Scilingo and the disappearances, the role of the military and the church, truth and justice, quickly occupied the center of the political debate in Argentina . . . ." [HV-2: 143] Although what Scilingo said may have taken most people by surprise, it was not news for the Mothers; as early as August 1977 they had read reports of the death flights in Rodolfo Walsh's underground newspaper.

Hebe was quick to take full advantage of Scilingo's confession and use it to revive interest in the disappeared. She focused on them in her speeches recalling the coup of 1976. In the course of her speeches, Hebe revealed that the Mothers had come to a new and more radical stage in their evolution. Here is part of the speech that Hebe gave in front of the Naval Mechanics School on March 23, 1995.

What Scilingo said is not news to us . . . . We knew about the penthonaval drug, we knew that they threw our children, while they were still alive, out of airplanes and into the sea . . . .

They made us live in terror, but they didn't succeed. They burned up our children with rubber tires and they didn't succeed, they buried them beneath the highways and still they didn't succeed . . . . Today, after so many years, our children return in each person who cries out, in each of you who protests.

We mothers, who took to the streets almost eighteen years ago, never imagined that today, in front of the Naval Mechanics School, this sinister place, we would say to you:

"Assassins, you sons of a thousand bitches, we hate you. We hate you from the very depths of our hearts. We hate you with the same strength with which we love our children . . . . We will never sit at your table because it is the table of the damned, of the assassins." [HM: 71-72]

That same day, Hebe spoke at the Law School of the University of Buenos Aires. Her speech reiterates old complaints and acknowledges that the Mothers have become revolutionaries.

Our speech in front of ESMA today was an act of vindication for our children. The military couldn't take our shouting at them the way we did. They came at us with nightsticks and billy clubs, which is the only thing they know how to do. But I just kept shouting at them that I hate them, that the whole world hates them . . . .

We will never allow them to try to repair with money what they must repair with justice. They want to give $100,000 to each mother. Imagine such an amount! And at a time like this when there's no money for education, none for the mothers of the Malvinas soldiers, none for health, none for books . . . . The lives of our children have no price. It is too great. There is not enough money in the whole world to ever pay for them.

We don't want the list of the dead; we want the list of the assassins. Do you know why they want to give us the list of the dead? Because death is final and that would put an end to it all for the government . . . . But we reject this from the very depths of our hearts. Our struggle has no end.

We went to the Naval Mechanics School today to tell the military that we will pursue them to the last day of our lives . . . . It is no small thing to be a revolutionary . . . . Nevertheless the Mothers feel that they are indeed revolutionaries. [HM: 75-80]

The following day, the nineteenth anniversary of the coup, Hebe spoke before a crowd in Neuquén, Argentina.

I am overwhelmed when I think about those beautiful bodies being thrown into the sea—those beautiful young girls exposed in their nakedness before the eyes of those gross sons of bitches. But what does it matter where they threw our children's bodies, where they buried them, where they burned them? Our children's ideas live on in our hearts and in the hearts of other young people today.

Nor does it matter how many times the military men strike us. They are not going to bring us to our knees because there are many of us mothers. If one mother falls there will be another and another and another. And new mothers, many of them young mothers, are coming along who are continuing the struggle so that their own children may live in a free country, in a just country . . . . [HM: 84-85]

# CHAPTER 14

## THE GOVERNMENT OF FERNANDO DE LA RÚA (1999-2001)

*Aggressive Militancy*

In October 1999, after ten years of Menem's rule, Fernando De La Rúa became the president of Argentina.

Hebe's stubborn militancy and explosive language were such that she and the Mothers were now beginning to be discredited, not just by the Argentine government, but also by human rights organizations. As the end of the twentieth century approached, it was evident that, besides being increasingly confirmed in their revolutionary tendencies, the Mothers had adopted an almost mystical relationship with their children.

Using the Mothers' newspaper to announce their plans for New Year's Eve in the Plaza de Mayo at the turn of the century, Hebe offered a glimpse of her transcendental view of that coming event.

On December 31, 1999 we will mark 1200 Thursdays of marching and twenty-two active, steadfast years as a great, immovable mountain, stoic in our principles and

convictions. . . . When the first bell of the millennium is
sounded, we will all join together in one single shout. At
that precise moment the miracle of transfusion will occur—
the transfusion of our children's blood to us and from us to
the new young revolutionaries of 2000. [MPM: Dec.1999,
p. 2]

On New Years Eve, 1999, in the Plaza de Mayo, it
seemed to happen as Hebe had imagined. The Mothers
and a great throng of people crowded into the Plaza de
Mayo where the pyramid was covered with pictures of
their disappeared children. Hebe reported that, "a strong
emotion took over the Plaza . . . our beloved and respected
revolutionaries, who gave birth to our combat, were there
with us in the Plaza de Mayo."

In the same December, 1999 newspaper, Hebe made
a number of radical statements. The first concerned her
new understanding of violence.

Many people don't have jobs, food for their children, a
house, water or gas. Where is the violence, compañeros, if
it is not in that situation? For someone to steal food because
he is hungry is much less of a crime than to break into a
bank . . . . I am convinced that it is only the government
that is violent. Our violence is necessary; they have brought
us to this place. [MPM: Dec. 1999, p.11]

Hebe also explained that the Mothers were losing their
student following because the Triple Alliance, (the old death
squad, the Mothers claimed, now under the new government
of President De La Rúa) had issued a warning to students:
"Don't go to the Plaza because there will be violence." But,
seemingly unfazed, at this point Hebe announced that the
Mothers had turned against the students. "Today our
compañeros are not the students but the unemployed workers.
Because the students of this city are petit bourgeois who

just follow behind the Triple Alliance so they can become servants of De La Rúa."

Hebe further stated that "the radical, difficult road taken by the Mothers is the only road" and that "political action is the best, the most marvelous action of man when it is done with love, with principles and with solidarity—as did our 30,000 beloved children who taught us." [MPM, Dec. 1999, p.13.].

In her most revealing declaration, Hebe acknowledged that the Mothers had a new and special weapon, a different weapon than "the truth", that they had spoken about in their early days. "This amazing weapon is the love of revolution, the love of transformation, the love of equality and socialism." [MPM: Dec. 1999, p.11]

## Conflicts, Threats and Responses

It was inevitable that conflicts between the Mothers and the government would continue at a high pitch. Hebe spoke out vehemently once again against the Triple Alliance. They, in their turn, began referring to her as "comandante guerrilla" and threatened her with death in a letter that came with a picture of the morgue. On the walls of the morgue, at Junin 700, was painted the message: "Death to Bonafini and the old women of the Plaza de Mayo." [MPM: Dec. 1999, p.22]. Hebe's response was direct and fearless, spoken like a hardened rebel.

Let them come look for me because I'm not going to hide. I am a Mother who shows her face and her body, and if they want to kill me, here I am. I don't hide because I'm not afraid of them. Because the person who fights and is killed for his people never dies, just as our children are never going to die, nor Che, nor all the compañeros who have given their lives. [MPM: Dec. 1999, p.11]

# The People's Revolutionary University

The Mothers' "love of revolution" manifested itself in a number of ways, but most concretely in the founding of an institution to train young revolutionaries. On April 6, 2000 the Mothers celebrated the opening of La Universidad Popular de las Madres de la Plaza de Mayo, combativa y revolutionaria (The People's University of the Mothers of the Plaza de Mayo, combative and revolutionary). For the Mothers, this new learning center not only represented a physical realization of "an astounding dream"; it was unmistakably the emotional, and mystical, embodiment of their disappeared children.

The Mothers visualized their university as something different from the usual university. They had no sympathy with private universities because they said that those centers of learning were not interested in changing the world, but in making money. Nor did the Mothers endorse public universities; they believed that such places were run for the benefit of the powerful men who controlled the economy, politics, the church and the military. Hebe firmly declared that the People's University would be both independent and Marxist.

This university is for the young people, and for others not so young, who have made up their minds to be prepared for this difficult road of the revolution . . . ." [MPM: April 2000, p.12]

Hebe added that it would be a place without the bourgeoisie or bureaucrats, without priests or nuns, a place for the people—the most unprotected people, the unemployed people who want to work but are not given work, the kids who want to study but are not able to, for those who believe in revolution and want to make Argentina a better country.

The only entrance requirement, Hebe stated, would be to know how to read and to love knowledge. Courses would be offered in such fields as social psychology, violence, human rights, journalism, art, television and theater, and the history of the Mothers of the Plaza de Mayo.

We are creating the University in order to establish schools where the children learn, as they do in Cuba, that the word "revolution", and the word "guerrilla", the words "solidarity" and "socialism" are the most tender of words, even sweeter than "love". [LL: June/July 2001, Supplement p. 7]

Hebe felt that the creation of this university brought the Mothers closer to their disappeared children. She saw the inauguration of the university as the birth of a new child, and, by extension, as the rebirth of their own children. She proclaimed that their children were in every step they had taken to make this university a reality. "The University is born great like our children, beautiful and free, just as they were born . . . . and here today we cut the cord and we present it to you, the people". [MPM: April, 2000, p.12]

So deep was the commitment of the People's University to revolution that Che Guevara was considered a model for the students and later, in 2002, the university created an Ernesto Che Guevara chair. Hebe's words at the inauguration of this chair convey her veneration for Che and the strong link she saw between him and the Mothers' children.

## More Radicalism

As further confirmation of their radical mode, the Mothers struck out against the United States, capitalism, imperialism and the World Bank. In an inflammatory statement, they denounced the national security policy, past and present, of the United States.

For fifty years a U. S. doctrine of national security was developed that implicated Argentina. This doctrine eventually spawned the savage Latin American dictatorships financed by the United States. With the excuse of combating terrorism, the United States and the World Bank planned the elimination of all political opposition and unleashed the worst genocide our lands have ever seen. Today the thing that endangers the imperialistic future is the millions of hungry, excluded people whom capitalism produced. Once again the United States and the World Bank are beginning to develop what they call the doctrine of national security. With the excuse now of combating drug traffic and terrorism, they are planning a new genocide and the violent repression of millions of marginal people living in Latin America. [MPM: May, 2000, p.9 ]

Hebe's outrage against the United States and the World Bank in no way dimmed her long-standing opposition to the Argentine government. About six months after De La Rúa became president, Hebe scornfully rejected any possibility of change in the Argentine political scene.

De La Rúa's party promised to be different, but they are the same and worse. Recently I told some journalists that the people in the new government will have a new wigmaker, even though they will not use the same wig. But within their heads they have the same shit and they will think the same. All the military are figureheads of the great multinationals who are the ones that pay for the political campaigns of De La Rúa and company. [MPM: April 20, 2000, p.23] .... De La Rúa's government is controlled by the most corrupt and criminal sectors of the "radical" party, the ones who supported the military dictatorship that made more than 30,000 of our children disappear. They are now finalizing plans to combat what they describe as "social lack of discipline" .... They only obey the dictates of the International Monetary Fund and are disposed to use the Armed Forces and Security to smother, with blood and fire, the protests of the people. [MPM: May, 2000, p.9]

## The Cuban Connection

The Mothers' decisive turn towards revolution was exemplified and greatly reinforced by Hebe's trip to Cuba to celebrate the anniversary of the Cuban revolution. The front page of the Mothers' newspaper for May 2000 had a picture of Fidel Castro embracing Hebe; in the background were hundreds of thousands of people who had gathered to mark the Cuban Revolution.

The Mothers' newspaper proudly proclaimed, "she thrilled the crowd with a profound and fiery speech." The following brief excerpts give the tone of the speech that Hebe delivered on May Day, 2000, to a huge crowd of Cuban people.

Comandante Fidel Castro, beloved compañeros, Cuban workers, Latin Americans—especially you, comandante, who today allow us to share this happy day. This is the best reward the Mothers have received in all of our 23 years of struggle. Thank you, beloved Cuban people, for letting us share this celebration of our revolution, of your revolution!

We are ashamed of Argentina's vote in the United Nations concerning human rights in Cuba. In my country human rights are violated every day, workers are beaten, people die of hunger, people are mercilessly assassinated, the prisons are concentration camps!

The Mothers believe in and love revolution—that revolution for which our children fought. Today we have opened a University for the formation of cadres who will surely shape the political strategies of this revolutionary road that the Mothers propose.

Cuba . . . is fighting for Elián and against the savage imperialism of the United States, the most accursed country, accursed its government, yes, accursed. We are not afraid of them and if we have to die in this struggle we do it with pride, as our children did. [MPM: May, 2000, p.11]

When all the speeches and celebrating finally came to an end, the Argentine delegation of the Mothers of the Plaza de Mayo had hoped that they might have ten or fifteen minutes to talk alone with Fidel Castro. Instead they talked with him until two o'clock in the morning, making a total of eight hours that Hebe spent with Castro.

After Hebe's visit to Cuba, the Mothers' pace, and rhetoric, took on a new intensity as their views on a variety of international issues, as well as their approach to problems in Argentina, became ever more radical and outspoken.

## Secretary of State Albright

In August 2000 when the United States Secretary of State, Madeleine Albright, visited Argentina, she met with representatives of seven groups, three of them human rights organizations, among them women from the Mothers of the Plaza de Mayo, including Hebe.

During the meeting Albright took a special interest in the disappeared and, as "a matter of conscience", pledged that she would try to persuade the U. S. government to declassify documents that might lead to more information about those who had disappeared during the Dirty War. To this statement of concerned commitment, Hebe's answer was "We do not believe her . . . It was hypocritical of Albright to say she is going to look into something that the government she represents was largely responsible for." [NYT: 8-17-2000]

## The ETA

Two months later Hebe created a major political disturbance by seeming to endorse the ETA, the violent Basque terrorist group that for many years has been fighting for the independence of the Basque region in Spain. The commotion began when the Association of Victims of Terrorism (AVT), a Spanish group protesting ETA terrorism, made public the contents of a document on the web page of the Mothers of the Plaza de Mayo registering their sympathy with the Basque people in the face of supposed persecution by the Spanish government. The Mothers document, signed by Hebe, specifically spoke of the detention, torture and executions of Basque people who were fighting for freedom from Spanish repression. The implication was clear that the Mothers considered the Spanish government to be guilty of criminal behavior, even of being a terrorist government. The Mothers also pointed their fingers at the Spanish judicial system that they accused of collaborating with the government. They turned on Judge Baltasar Garzón, whom they denounced for his firm stand against the ETA.

The response of the public, both in Spain and in Argentina, was pronounced. The website document was widely interpreted as an unmistakable indication that the Mothers of the Plaza de Mayo now countenanced violence as a means to a political end.

The Spanish government did not take the Mothers' accusations lightly. The Mothers of the Plaza de Mayo was denounced in Spain; its members were characterized in the press as evil-minded, ignorant women, and were declared "persona non grata". The Spanish Minister of the Interior declared that the Mothers of the Plaza de Mayo had a distorted, false and profoundly unjust view of Spanish society and warned that if the Mothers did not retract its statements on ETA it would do itself very great harm.

In a telephone call to Hebe, the AVT asked the Mothers not only to withdraw its statement on ETA but also to apologize to the AVT. Hebe's answer was simple and direct. She said that she didn't need to ask anyone's pardon — and then she abruptly hung up.

In Buenos Aires there was also sharp criticism of the Mothers and their stand on ETA; about 500 people demonstrated to show their concerned disapproval of the Mothers. Among their critics were representatives of the Founding Line of the Mothers of the Plaza de Mayo who emphasized that, while they had been part of the original Mothers' group, they had broken off from the group in 1986 because they disagreed with the authoritarian views of Hebe de Bonafini and some of her followers. Their letter enunciated firmly that all the women in the Mothers' movement did not share Hebe's opinions about ETA and that the Mothers of the Founding Line were averse to using violence to settle political differences and instead favored resolution by peaceful processes. The Grandmothers of the Plaza de Mayo also expressed apprehension about Hebe and debated whether she had become "crazy and dictatorial".

*La Nación* summed up the Spanish reaction to Hebe's endorsement of ETA with this one sentence; "In a single day the group that Hebe de Bonafini leads risked all the essential support that it had counted on in Spain for so many years." [*La Nación*: Oct. 28, 2000] By then it was clear that the Mothers of the Plaza de Mayo were continuing to lose support in Argentina too.

Other reactions to the Mothers' support of the ETA were quick in coming. The president of the Spanish section of Amnesty International wrote Hebe stating that the crimes of the ETA had made a mockery of humanitarian principles and the dictates of the public conscience. A letter written by Ernesto Sábato, the director of CONADEP, proclaimed, "the dishonest interests of ETA should be repudiated by all of us who have a genuine conviction about the sacred quality of human life . . ." [*El Mundo*: Nov. 4, 2000]

The Mothers who had for years condemned the killing and torture of their children by the Argentine military junta, were now endorsing and supporting the same crimes if they were done for what the Mothers regarded as worthy ends. The end, now, seemed to justify the means.

## Las Locas

The Mothers' chief means of communication, their newspaper, took a completely new form in December of 2000, eight months after Hebe's trip to Cuba, when the first issue of *Las Locas* appeared. Replacing their modest publication on ordinary newsprint, the Mothers presented themselves in an over-sized, rather sophisticated, magazine of some forty pages printed on high quality paper. The cover of this first issue features a painting in seven colors, entitled "Globalization". It depicts four scowling people (two men and two women) under an American flag. Beside the flag is a man, quite possibly intended to portray the financier George Soros.

On the slick paper of the back cover of *Las Locas*, Hebe has a full page essay entitled "Resisting with Dreams and Hopes" where she talks about the Resistance March to be held on December 6 and 7, 2001.

In December of 2001, we will make our twentieth annual Resistance March and we will reflect on our dreams and hopes. The march will be dedicated to our children, and above all to those enslaved children and adults who are condemned to prostitute themselves as the only way to bring money to their families. We will dedicate our march to them as a denunciation of such large-scale perversion. While businessmen, military officers and politicians raise their glasses with hands dripping with jewels (the products of robbery, exploitation and genocide), there are millions of children who are dying without ever having known love, tenderness, a toy or a book. While people are consumed with their soulless greed, most of the people on this planet will be crying from hunger. They will be sick and marginalized, enslaved in the mines of Africa or on the streets of the great cities of our Third World.

Our rallying cry will be: **The future has arrived, help us to change it.** This shout should reach into every corner of this planet that is full of misery, but also full of men, women and children who are not resigned to live on their knees, although they are now living the wretched lives of worms. LL, December 2000]

## Stand Against Globalization

One of the Mothers' first acts in the new century was to enlarge their sphere of concern by taking an active stand against globalization. At the end of January, 2001, when 5,000 activist delegates met in Brazil to raise their voices against capitalism, imperialism and free world trade, Hebe was there as a representative of the Mothers of the Plaza de Mayo.

One of the unique features of this meeting was to have been a live debate, via satellite, between members of the World Economic Forum, (the elite of the world economy, meeting in Davos, Switzerland) and the World Social Forum (opponents of globalization, meeting in Puerto Alegre, Brazil). The apparent underlying purpose of the videobridge on that January 28, 2001 was to initiate a dialogue that would help to define an economic alternative to "unfettered capitalism".

Unfortunately the dialogue turned into a shouting match between the billionaire financier, George Soros, and Hebe. The videobridge was a resounding failure. The trouble started when Mr. Soros was understandably unable to answer the question of how many Third World children die daily in abject misery. At that tense moment Hebe started yelling at Mr. Soros, "You people are our enemies, you are a hypocrite." She made matters even worse by shouting out at him "You monster!" [EN-O Soros] To which Soros responded, "I am looking at your face and all I can do is smile. You have broken off all dialogue. We were prepared to open a dialogue with you." [*Associated Press*, Jan. 28, 2001] For the time there appeared to be no possibility of bringing opposing points of views on globalization into a meaningful discussion.

## The Zapatistas

The Mothers had been supporters of the Zapatista movement in Chiapas, Mexico ever since its violent 1994 uprising. Late in February 2001, in a dramatic reversal of intent, the Zapatistas, under the leadership of Subcomandante Marcos, signaled their interest in opening a dialogue with the Mexican government that might end seven years of conflict and bring about an Indian bill of rights. Subcomandante Marcos, their controversial chief, led 23 ski-masked followers on a peaceful two week "March for Dignity" to Mexico City. The marchers were unarmed, but were accompanied by supporters and human rights monitors.

By the time the Zapatistas arrived in Mexico City in mid March, peace was balancing on a tenuous thread. The newly elected President of Mexico, Vicente Fox, had been conciliatory and had shown genuine signs of wanting to negotiate with the rebels. However Marcos had his doubts about the sincerity of Fox's peace offerings.

A week later, Hebe was also in Mexico City and met with Zapatista leaders. She warned them to be wary of the Mexican government, saying that she didn't trust President Fox. "Presidents are hypocrites, like the one we have there in Argentina." Then she announced that she believed that it was not yet time for the rebels to lay down their arms for good "because governments are very, very traitorous and they never carry out what they promise." [*Reforma*: Mexico City, March 15, 2001]

In June, Marcos visited the Mothers in Buenos Aires. Hebe told him that "the struggle of the Zapatistas is the struggle of the Mothers, it is our struggle and we feel as Zapatista as Marcos because we feel the struggle as our own." [LL: June 2001, Supplement, p. 7]

## Twenty-five years after the coup

While the Mothers were becoming ever more openly revolutionary, there were signs that one of the goals that had given purpose to their lives ever since the days of the Dirty War might be achieved. The time seemed to be approaching when the military responsible for the deaths of their children might be brought to trial.

On March 24, 2001, the 25th anniversary of the coup, the *New York Times* printed an editorial entitled "Delayed Justice in Argentina", that said in part:

> Today marks the 25th anniversary of Argentina's last successful military coup, which brought to power a junta whose murderous repression of Argentina's peaceful left became known as the "dirty war". It is a sign of Argentina's growing confidence as a democracy that some of the soldiers and mid-level officers responsible for the abuses may soon be brought to trial.
>
> After Argentina returned to democracy in 1983, the government, under threat from the military, issued an amnesty for crimes committed by all but the top officers. But earlier this month, a judge declared these laws illegal, ruling that the crimes were so serious

that they could not be forgiven and that the amnesties violated international treaties Argentina had signed.

The ruling, which has been appealed to the Supreme Court, has won widespread praise in Argentina, but also opposition from powerful quarters. Military officers have condemned it, as have civilian government officials. . . .

If Judge Cavallo's decision is upheld in Argentina, it could lead to a long-overdue removal from the military of those with complicity in the dirty war. Trials would also finally provide relief for some of the tens of thousands of those who were tortured or who lost family members, victims whose suffering is as fresh as it was a generation ago. Argentina has changed dramatically since 1976. It is now a full democracy with no fear of a military coup. There is no longer a reason to avoid the justice that Argentina deserves. [NYT: March 24, 2001]

This editorial radiated real hope. Unfortunately such action may have come too late for the Mothers. By then the Mothers had given up on the Argentine judicial system and had committed themselves to doctrinaire revolutionary positions. They had come a long, long way since their early days of innocence and were now embarked on an outspoken course that promised to be in continual conflict with governmental authority, and close to the outright endorsement of terrorism.

## Hebe's Reaction to 9/11

Just how fundamental Hebe's change has been is sadly reflected in her response to the September 11th attack on the World Trade Center. Hebe was in Cuba on September 11th, 2001, but soon after her return to Argentina she gave a speech at the People's University of the Mothers of the

Plaza de Mayo. Her words confirm her thorough hatred for the United States and her ready acceptance of violence. "I am not going to be a hypocrite; it didn't make me at all sad." For Hebe, this act of terrorism "avenged the blood of so many people", including presumably, her own two sons. She likened the authors of the attacks to the Mothers' revolutionary children when she flatly stated that the perpetrators of the terrorist acts of September 11, 2001 "were courageous men and women who were prepared for what they did and gave their lives for us. They declared war with their bodies, crashing their planes into the towers and making shit of the greatest power in the world. And this made me happy." [HV-3: 10.1.01]

To even attempt to fathom the strangeness and horror of Hebe's statement, it may help to contemplate the observation of Alberto Granado, one of Che Guevara's best friends, who noted the difference between the two men in their outlook on face-to-face warfare: "Che could look through a sniperscope at a soldier and pull the trigger, knowing that by killing him he was helping reduce repression—'saving 30,000 future lives from hunger'— whereas when [I, Granado] looked through the scope, [I] saw a man with a wife and children." [JLA: 571]

# CODA II

## THE MOTHERS AS SEEN IN 2003

The Mothers of the Plaza de Mayo have changed radically since they first formed as a group in 1977. Although they once deservedly elicited an outpouring of sympathy from supporters of human rights and were held up as models for women's peaceful protest movements, they have now lost their mainstream approval.

The fundamental transformation of the Mothers' movement compels a rethinking of our perception of them. The earlier, possibly romanticized image of a group of gritty, middle-aged women tirelessly walking around the Plaza de Mayo and peacefully protesting the disappearance of their children must now be replaced by one that is shaped by the reality of a group of mostly old women engaged in a variety of revolutionary activities that support their alliances, even to the point of endorsing violence and terrorism as a means to their ends.

To attempt to understand the Mothers' transformation, it is useful to review what it was that initially drove them and what impelled them to change their course.

First and foremost, throughout nearly a quarter of a century, is the Mothers' relationship with their children. They were mostly women of little education who found their satisfactions in their homes and families. Hebe's story reflects a sense of warm, mutual affection between her and her sons. The Mothers' devotion to their children is genuine and at first manifests itself in the belief in their innocence of anything that might have justified their detention. The longing to keep their children's memories alive and to feel closer to them, as well as to vindicate them, helps to explain why (when they finally realized that their children had been militant revolutionaries) the Mothers tried to follow in what they conceived to be their children's footsteps—even to becoming followers of Che Guevara's revolutionary political philosophy.

A significant aspect of the Mothers' evolution is their growing disdain for governments. If the Argentine government, aided and abetted by the military, and all too often supported by the upper reaches of the Catholic Church, had never become involved in using such horrendous measures to suppress subversives, the Mothers would never have had reason to be formed. And if government forces had not maintained a veil of secrecy and a stubborn pursuit of immunity for all the military, the Mothers might not have taken the revolutionary steps that have brought them to where they are today.

From 1977 to 1983 the Mothers' frustration was focused on the total lack of government cooperation in accounting for thousands of disappearances. Their despair was heightened by the full realization of the horrors of the detention centers. Then followed the letdown after the military trials in 1985 and the sense that most of the perpetrators of the crimes against their children would never be brought to justice. In 1990 when President Menem pardoned the few men who had been convicted in 1985, the Mothers protested, but to no avail, and they were forced to realize that there was little likelihood that they would ever be able to successfully combat the military's presumption of impunity.

It was at this point that the Mothers turned to other causes, causes that they thought their children, in their hopes of building a better world, would have endorsed. These causes frequently used the rhetoric of revolution; some of them condoned violence.

By 1990 the Mothers had lost their original innocence and assumed a more calculated and aggressive approach to the world. Because dialogue, negotiation and the exploration of reconciliation were never among the Mothers' tools, Hebe maintained that protesting and resisting were the only ways to solve their problems.

The Mothers' early emphasis on non-violent protest weakened further after Hebe's visit to Cuba in May of 2000 and their rhetoric became much more combative on behalf of the causes they endorsed. Hebe's language began to incorporate such phrases as "this obscene capitalist system", "the accursed United States government", and "Argentina is so full of shit". Her language after the World Trade Center attack explicitly endorsed violence.

Central to the Mothers' movement at all times is Hebe who, perhaps amazingly, goes on and on — speaking, traveling, and now helping to guide the People's University. Her leadership of the Mothers of the Plaza de Mayo began with Azucena's death in 1977 and has been the dominant force that has kept the Mothers active and has propelled them in new directions. Hebe, of course, did not do this alone and there have been many, many other Mothers marching and working for their common goals. But it is only the voice of Hebe that an English-speaking audience hears and hers is the prominent presence in every picture of the Mothers. It is the name Hebe de Bonafini that is identified with the Mothers' movement and has become known far beyond Argentina.

Hebe's relationship with Jorge and Raúl, her early alliance with the working class, her lack of humility and her total fearlessness have all been important in her relentless pursuit of the Mothers' goals. She has declared that the Mothers will never give up, that they will give the government no rest, and that, as long as they are alive, their children will never die.

Hebe's blunt words after the terrorist attack of September 11th suggest that she felt that the disappearances and deaths of the Mothers' children had been avenged by the lives lost at the World Trade Center. She has been comfortable with the terrorists' bold revolutionary stance and evidently considered that the attack was legitimate. But to most of those who know about those words, they seem grossly unacceptable. Today Hebe, once a widely admired figure, has become a person to be repudiated, even a person to be scorned.

In 2001 three significant examples decisively demonstrate the revolutionary turn that the Mothers have taken. The most important is Hebe's astounding expression of happiness on hearing about the terrorist attack on the United States. A second is that the white kerchief that was for so many people around the world a symbol of peaceful protest has now become, as Hebe told the Zapatista Subcomandante Marcos, "not the symbol of pacifism but of revolution". [LL, June/July, 2001, Supplement, p. 7] A third is that the Plaza de Mayo that had always been for the Mothers a sacred, almost mystical, place where they sensed the presence of their children, has become in the Mothers' minds a place "not just inhabited by the disappeared but also by those who feel the revolution in their blood". [op. cit., p.4]]

As the story of the evolution of the Mothers of the Plaza de Mayo now reaches its disconcerting conclusion, it is saddening to reflect that at a moment when there is real hope that the guilty Argentine military may finally be brought to justice, the Mothers of the Plaza de Mayo have squandered the goodwill for which they fought so hard and have turned their backs on orderly processes of law. They appear to have severely damaged their reputation as models of non-violent protest. With these losses, the long-term potential of their movement, once so promising, has also been squandered. However appealing the early image of Mothers of the Plaza de Mayo may have been, it no longer deserves to be perpetuated.

The path of the Mothers' evolution in the last two decades should serve as a cautionary tale, but it should in no way tarnish the importance of the Mothers' early triumph of courageously breaking the paralysis of silence by marching, Thursday after Thursday after Thursday, in peaceful protest during Argentina's Dirty War. This is the Mothers' proud legacy. Notwithstanding the most recent phases of their movement, it is a legacy of continuing significance.

# ENDNOTES

## Endnote A, p. 22: Sarmiento

Domingo Faustino Sarmiento (1811-1888) is a towering figure in Argentine history. A statesman and foreign diplomat, educator and writer, he was President from 1868 to 1874. His career was dedicated to building a new, progressive Argentina modeled on practices in Europe, and especially, in the United States.

Education was of great interest to Sarmiento. While he was representing Argentina in Washington from 1865-68 he traveled extensively around the United States learning as much as he could that might be usefully applied to Argentina. He was greatly influenced by the progressive pedagogical approach of Horace Mann and by the ideals of democracy

## Endnote B, p. 23: Moreno

A lawyer and an intellectual, Mariano Moreno (1778-1811) was an important political figure in Argentina's struggle for independence from Spain. When Spanish forces were driven out of the country, he briefly took part in the new Argentine government. Moreno is known for being a strong proponent of free trade and for having founded both the first library in Argentina and the first Buenos Aires newspaper.

## Endnote C, p. 35: Operación Masacre

*Operación Masacre* is Rodolfo Walsh's detailed and disturbing report on the deaths (in a dump in the suburbs of Buenos Aires) of suspected Perónists after an uprising on June 9, 1956. Excerpts from this chilling account of the massacre appear for the first time in English translation in the *Argentina Reader*. [AR:333-339] In retrospect these macabre events of 1956 seem to be the harbinger of what was to happen with stunning frequency during the Dirty War.

## Endnote D, p. 42: "Che" Guevara

In the 1960's, the political climate in Argentina, as in many parts of the globe, was in a state of turbulent flux. Revolutionary ideas such as Che expressed in an essay written in 1962 during the Cuban missile crisis resonated with students all over the world. A few powerful lines from that essay convey the seriousness with which Che proposed the concept of a Latin American revolution based on the Cuban model. Perhaps most significant is Che's conclusion that, in the global struggle between imperialism and socialism, there appeared to be little possibility of a peaceful solution—no way to avert terrifying violence and loss of lives.

"Is it possible or not, given the present conditions in our continent, to achieve it by peaceful means? We emphatically answer that, in the great majority of cases, this is not possible."

"What is the history of Cuba if it is not the history of Latin America? And what is the history of Latin America if it is not the history of Asia, Africa and Oceania? And what is the history of all these peoples if it is not the history of the most merciless and cruel imperialistic exploitation in the modern world?"

"In many Latin American countries revolution is inevitable . . . . Today's restlessness is an unmistakable symptom of rebellion."

""The blood of the people is our most valued treasure, but it must be used in order to save more blood in the future." [AR: 345-351]

## Endnote E, p. 45: Torture

Despicable, degrading and extremely painful tortures were inflicted on the disappeared. The most obvious reasons for such torture were breaking the victim in order to get "confessions" and to learn the identify of other "subversives". But not to be overlooked was the exhilaration the torturer could feel as he had complete control of his helpless victim.

Most tortures ended in death. However there were frequently doctors present who would try to prevent the victim from dying if he, or often she, was on the verge of confessing. Those who broke and revealed useful information were "rehabilitated" so that, for example, they could help with the running of the ESMA newspaper. More chillingly, captives turned informants were sometimes assigned to ride around the streets in the back of vans and "mark" people they knew might be considered "subversives". These fresh victims would then be picked up, tortured and, usually, killed.

The torture most often reported was the use of "la picana", an electric cattle prod, skillfully applied to every part of the body, especially the most sensitive places.

Rape and obscene abuse of female prisoners frequently occurred.

Subtler forms of torture were shouted insults and humiliation, and the unnerving blare of radios turned to their highest pitch. Or conversely, there was the torment of the utter silence of solitary confinement. In a similar way, deprivation of light by keeping prisoners constantly blindfolded or its reverse, subjecting them to the glare of intense light, was also used to bring prisoners to the breaking point.

*Nunca Más* described the tortures used during the Dirty War as "licensed sadism"—a description that is borne out by the brief excerpts from that work in *The Argentina Reader*. [AR:440-447].

## Endnote F, p. 46: The Media

Horatio Verbitsky, Argentina's leading investigative journalist, reports that after 1955, although restrictions on the press were expected, "no aspect of official politics was safe from the scrutiny of the press." In the 1960's "it was still possible to publish analysis and accusations in a paper written, printed, distributed and sold in the light of day." [HV-1: 5] But after the coup of 1976, the junta made a determined effort to silence the media and use it to its own advantage.

Television stations were tightly controlled by the military and used to put out disinformation or official propaganda. Argentine radio stations were similarly controlled. Only one voice dared to speak out: from a Uruguayan station with transmission studios in Buenos Aires: Ariel Delgado broadcast early every morning and noontime in an attempt to keep the Argentine people informed.

The press was so severely muffled that it was impossible to either cover or criticize the atrocious things that the military was doing. Most Buenos Aires newspapers were sympathetic with the goals of the junta or at least went along with the silencing of the press. With few exceptions, they did not rise up in opposition to the military regime nor question its legitimacy. *La Opinión* and the English *Buenos Aires Herald* were the only newspapers to even publish the names of the disappeared. The military government expropriated *La Opinión*; its editor, Jacobo Timerman, a defender of freedom of the press, was imprisoned, tortured, held under house arrest for 30 months and finally expelled from Argentina. The editor of the *Herald*, Robert Cox, was arrested and later released, but only on the condition that he leave the country.

However there were many individual journalists who were not willing to cooperate with the muzzling of the press; they literally put their lives on the line. In the seven years of the dictatorship, close to 100 members of the press were themselves disappeared and presumed killed.

Among them was the courageous Rodolfo Walsh, a writer and journalist with a long history of going against the political tide. He reacted strongly to the repression and struck out with the written word against the brutality of the junta. For it was his belief that people should not give in to the terror, that the only way to survive was to keep people informed by means of a clandestine press.

In June of 1976 Walsh started a cable service called ANCLA, an acronym for Agency for Clandestine News. For over a year, ANCLA cables were sent to editors and correspondents of international publications and in this way alerted a larger world with the first accusations against the junta.

On December 1, 1976, once again putting his convictions into action, Walsh began circulating an underground newspaper, *Cadena Informativa*. Working alone on his typewriter, he wrote the copy himself; it was distributed once or twice a month by his friends and colleagues. To those daring few, he said: "Get this information out however you can—by hand, by machine or by mimeograph. Send copies to your friends. Nine out of ten people will be waiting for it. Millions want to be informed. Terror is founded on a lack of communication. Break the isolation." [Ibid: 38]

## Endnote G, p. 46: Amnesty International

The junta's treatment of Amnesty International (AI) during their fact-finding trip to Argentina in 1976 is revealing. Observers from Amnesty International were the object of one of the largest intelligence operations ever mounted in Argentina. An Argentine surveillance team of roughly 100 men, given the code name "Operation Christmas", was established with headquarters in the Hotel President where the North American priest, Robert Drinan, and English members of the team, Lord Averbury and Patricia

Feeney, were staying. Microphones were hidden in their rooms, their papers and documents were secretly photographed, and everyone who approached them was recorded on film.

While AI team members were given complete freedom of movement in Argentina, they could only exercise this freedom under the restrictions of an unrequested escort of 6 automobiles, 1 motorcycle, roughly 100 policemen and a van with a hidden camera. The only people who had a chance to talk with the observers were some foreign correspondents, a small number of foreign diplomats and a few sanitized politicians. [HV-1: 74-75]

## Endnote H, p.61: Mignone

Hebe later learned that the "Emilio" who spoke to her at the detention center was Emilio Mignone, a distinguished lawyer who during the Dirty War founded and directed the Center for Legal and Social Studies, a human rights group that attempted to make the military take responsibility for the kidnappings, tortures and murder that were occurring in Argentina.

Early in the morning of May 14, 1976, armed men came to his house and arrested his twenty-four year old daughter, Monica. Mr. Mignone recalled how he told his daughter to go with the men, who showed army identification, saying that he would seek her release in court. At that time the large number of disappearances was not widely known, and Mignone, a devout Roman Catholic and a Peronist, had faith in due process. He never saw his daughter again.

Monica Mignone had been active in a volunteer group of Catholics who were working among the slum dwellers of Buenos Aires. Mr. Mignone and his wife, Angelica, spent weeks going to courts and ministries and meeting with high military authorities. They contacted church officials, and again they felt spurned. Despite writs of habeas corpus, they never learned what happened to their daughter.

## Endnote I, p. 70: Plaza de Mayo

Since 1810 when protests focused on freeing Argentina from Spanish rule, the Plaza de Mayo has been the historical, political and emotional heart of Buenos Aires. The Plaza is surrounded by the Government House, the Casa Rosada, (the Argentine White House), the Metropolitan Cathedral (dating from 1784), and the National Bank. In the center of the plaza is the Pyramid of Mayo, built in 1811 to commemorate the first anniversary of the May Revolution. It was refurbished in 1856 and a statue of liberty was placed on top of it. Walkways, gardens and palm trees make the plaza a favorite place for people to gather in Buenos Aires.

In its earliest days the Plaza de Mayo was the place where public processions started, where elaborate religious celebrations were held and where dances, fireworks and illuminations gave a festive tone to the young city. Over the years, presidents have often delivered speeches to great crowds from the balcony of the Casa Rosada. In the 1950's adoring workers came there to hear Eva Perón speak.

It seems no accident that the Mothers chose to take their defiant stand against the government in this highly visible center of Buenos Aires.

## Endnote J, p. 100: Astiz

Gustavo Nino was in no way "the Blonde Angel" that the Mothers had fondly called him. He was, in bold fact, the 27 year old Naval Captain Alfredo Astiz, a member of the infamous Naval Task Force 3.3.2, notorious for its acts of kidnapping, torture and murder.

In October of 1977, Astiz infiltrated the Mothers' group by telling them that he was a student from Mar del Plata whose brother had disappeared. It was he who helped to set up the sting operation at the Santa Cruz Church on December 8, 1977, he who "fingered" the French nun, Alice Domon, he who two days later was responsible for the death of the French nun, Leonie Duquet, he who planned the abduction of Azucena Villaflor de Vicenti. Astiz excelled in kidnapping, torturing and killing women, none of them proven terrorists.

Tina Rosenberg gives an in-depth profile of him in her book *Children of Cain: Violence and the Violent in Latin America.*

In 1987 Astiz was held for five months but was released because of the Amnesty Laws that pardoned those who committed crimes while "following orders". At a trial in Paris in 1990 he was sentenced, in absentia, to life imprisonment for the deaths of the two French nuns, Alice Domon and Leonie Duquet. But at that time Astiz himself was free in Argentina and this sentence only meant that he was not able to leave his country for fear that Interpol would arrest him.

In July 2001, Astiz, by then retired as a naval officer due to public protest and pressure from the French, surrendered to police on charges of having kidnapped three Italian citizens during the Dirty War. The Italian government wanted to extradite him to Italy but the Argentine government has refused to comply, saying that his crimes should be judged by the judicial system of his own country. Astiz, at this writing, is still eluding justice and remains free in Argentina.

## Endnote K, p. 119: The OAS Visit

Throughout the OAS investigation, the Argentine government appeared to give its full cooperation to the OAS Commission. The Commission met with major figures from a great variety of organizations: governmental, religious, human rights, trade union, business, university, student and the media. It also met with former presidents of Argentina as well as with Ernesto Sábato and Jacobo Timerman. Members visited major cities in the country; from the general public they received 5580 denunciations of the regime.

Despite the efforts of the military junta to cover up the abuses of the Dirty War, the OAS Commission was not fooled in its investigation of September 6-20, 1979. Their report was not a "white wash" but reflected carefully thought-out critical observations about the human rights situation in Argentina from 1975 to 1979. The Commission understood that there was provocation in the form of terrorism from both the right and left, but they also began to comprehend, at first hand, the awful truth of the kidnapping, torture and killings. From there it was a short step to acknowledging that the provoking acts of terrorism were overshadowed by the government's "attempts to suppress subversion by dispensing with all moral and legal considerations." [OAS:134] With this realization, the Commission recognized that the Argentine government considered combating terrorism to be much more important than protecting human rights.

The Commission cited the abuse of fundamental human rights and issued recommendations aimed at trying to punish the guilty, but they had no power to enforce their words. The Argentine government could, and did, just politely deny their charges and recommendations. In the end the Commission had to confess its frustration and its failure to make any changes in the pattern of "serious, generalized and systematic violation of basic human rights and freedoms." [OAS: p.1]

The 374-page OAS report was published in the United States in 1980. Although the junta refused to release it, Emilio Mignone succeeded in smuggling 200 copies of it into Argentina. The OAS report lives on and makes for important reading.

## Endnote L, p: 122: The Grandmothers of the Plaza de Mayo

Babies and children were sometimes "disappeared" at the time one or both of their "subversive" parents were abducted. This was all part of a plan both to assure that subversion would not be carried into the next generation and also to provide children for childless couples.

The Grandmothers of the Plaza de Mayo was formed in 1977 by a group of grandmothers desperately trying to find the disappeared children of their own children. These women have marched and protested much as the Mothers have and they have also found support internationally, especially from Canada and Europe.

Genetic testing of blood has been partially successful in identifying many of the missing children who had been located in adopted homes. Although arranging for the legal return of these children involves a long and difficult legal struggle, it continues still.

Rita Arditti has written an informative book on this subject, *The Grandmothers of the Plaza de Mayo and the Disappeared Children of Argentina*. The film, *The Official Story*, gives a fictionalized version of the problem, as does the engrossing novel, *Tales from the Blue Archives* by Lawrence Thornton.

## Endnote M, p. 123: Euphemisms

The junta used language creatively in an attempt to conceal what they were actually doing. The most obvious of those euphemisms is the word "disappeared" which implies someone has mysteriously vanished forever. It really meant someone who had been kidnapped and surely detained. The frequent, and final, interpretation of "disappeared" is "dead."

To say someone would be "transferred" meant that the person would be taken away and killed.

In answer to Verbitsky's query "You're saying that all navy officers participated in *kidnapping, torture*, and *clandestine executions?*" Scilingo corrected him by answering "the entire navy participated in *detentions, interrogations, and the elimination of subversives . . . .*" [HV-2: 35-36, italics added].

Marguerite Feitlowitz studied "the verbal atrocities of the regime" and has written an impressive book on this subject, *A Lexicon of Terror*.

## Endnote N, p. 164: Exhumations

Exhumation is now widely accepted as a first step in the forensic study of the skeletal remains of the victims of crimes against humanity. Of immediate importance and possible comfort to the victims' families, is the returning of the remains of a loved one so there can be burial with religious rites. More basically, forensic anthropology has had significant impact as a means of exposing mass crimes and unearthing evidence to be used in human rights tribunals.

In 1984, the Argentine National Commission on Disappeared Persons sponsored a team of forensic scientists from the United States headed by Clyde C. Snow, to work in Argentina and to train Argentine students. The group came under the auspices of the American Association of the Advancement of Science and was financed by the Ford Foundation. The Argentine team eventually found more than 500 skeletons. Mr. Snow presented a dramatic slide show as testimony in the 1985 trial of nine top junta members.

Tina Rosenberg recently commented, "As advances in the use of DNA allow easier identification of remains and as trials for human rights abuses become more widespread, exhumations will be even more valuable for exposing—and thus helping to deter— mass killings. Murderers can count on eliminating or intimidating witnesses. Even years later, however, forensic anthropology can make eloquent and effective testimony from the silence of the dead." [NYT: editorial page, April 4, 2000.]

## Endnote O, p: 195: Soros

After Hebe called Soros a "monster", an interviewer asked her what she saw in Soros' face on the video that made her call him that. She answered: "Everything. Hunger, unemployment, Rwanda, our children dying, the slums of Brazil and Argentina, desperation". Then Hebe added, "You see him and you want to vomit. He is a worthless, repugnant person. He doesn't have the face of a human being." [*Noticias* March 17, 2001.]

The *Current Biography Yearbook*, 1997, gives a very different assessment of Mr. Soros: He was born in Budapest in 1934, was educated at the London School of Economics and has become an extremely successful investment banker and philanthropist who has given well over a billion dollars to promote just, democratic societies around the world.

The Soros Foundation has also had a strong impact in the United States where funds have been devoted to the causes of prison reform, the legalization of the medical use of marijuana, needle exchange programs and the care of the dying.

The new biography of Soros by Michael T. Kaufman gives an impressive measure of the man and his philanthropic outreach.

# SELECTED BIBLIOGRAPHY

Agosin, Marjorie. *The Mothers of The Plaza de Mayo (Linea Fundadora): The Story of Renée Epelbaum, 1976-1985*. Translated by Janice Molloy. Trenton, NJ: The Red Sea Press, 1990.

Anderson, Jon Lee. *Che Guevara: A Revolutionary Life*. New York: Grove Press, 1997.

Arditti, Rita. *Searching for Life: The Grandmothers of the Plaza de Mayo and the Disappeared Children of Argentina*. Berkeley: University of California Press, 1999.

Bonafini, Hebe de. *Historias de Vida*. Buenos Aires: Gráficos Talgraf, 1985.

Bouvard, Marguerite Guzman. *Revolutionizing Motherhood: The Mothers of the Plaza de Mayo*. Wilmington: Scholarly Resources, 1994.

Castro-Klarén, *Sara,* Sylvia Molloy and Beatriz Sarlo, Eds. *Women's Writing in Latin America: An Anthology*. Boulder: Westview Press, 1991.

Corbatta, Jorgelina. *Narrativas de La Guerra Sucia en Argentina*. Buenos Aires: Corregidor, 1999.

Diago, Alejandro. *Hebe de Bonafini: Memoria y esperanza*. Buenos Aires: Ediciones Dialéctica, 1988.

Elkin, Judith Laikin. "Recoleta: Civilization and Barbarism in Argentina." *Michigan Quarterly Review* (Spring 1988): 221-239.

Feitlowitz, Marguerite. *A Lexicon of Terror: Argentina and the Legacies of Torture*. New York: Oxford, 1998.

Fisher, Jo. *Mothers of the Disappeared*. Boston: South End Press, 1989.

Foster, David William. *Violence in Argentine Literature*. Columbia, MO: University of Missouri Press, 1995.

Guillermoprieto, Alma. *Looking for History: Dispatches from Latin America*. New York: Pantheon Books, 2001.

*Historia de Las Madres de Plaza de Mayo*. Buenos Aires: Ediciones Madres de Plaza de Mayo, 1995.

Kaufman, Michael T. *Soros: The Life and Time of a Messianic Billionaire*, New York: Alfred A Knopf, 2002.

Mellibovsky, Matilde. *Circle of Love over Death: Testimonies of the Mothers of the Plaza de Mayo*. Translated by Maria and Matthew Proser. Willimantic, CT: Curbstone Press, 1997.

Mignone, Emilio. *Iglesia and dictadura*. Buenos Aires: Ediciones del Pensamiento Nacional, 1986.

Nouzeilles, Gabriela and Graciela Montaldo, Eds. *The Argentina Reader: An Anthology*. Durham: Duke University Press, 2002.

*Nunca Más: The Report of the Argentine National Commission on the Disappeared*. New York: Farrar Straus, and Giroux, 1986.

Organization of American States, International Commission on Human Rights. *Report of the Situation of Human Rights in Argentina, 1980*.

Partnoy, Alice. *The Little School: Tales of Disappearance and Survival in Argentina*. Pittsburgh: Cleis Press, 1986.

*Rodolfo Walsh*. Madrid: Ediciones Rescate: Serie de los trabajadores de la cultura represaliados en la Argentina, 1981.

Rosenberg, Tina. *Children of Cain: Violence and the Violent in Latin America*. New York: William Morrow, 1991.

Shirer, William L. *Gandhi: A Memoir*. New York: Washington Square Press, 1982.

Taylor, Diane. *Disappearing Acts*. Durham: Duke University Press, 1997.

Timerman, Jacobo. *Prisoner without a Name, Cell without a Number*. (Translated by Toby Talbot). New York: Vintage Press, 1988.

Verbitsky, Horacio. *Rodolfo Walsh y la prenza clandestina (1976-1978)*. Buenos Aires: Ediciones de la Urraca, 1985.

—*The Flight: Confessions of an Argentine Dirty Warrior*. (Translated by Esther Allen). New York: New Press, 1996.

Walsh, Rodolfo. *El violento oficio de escribir*. Buenos Aires: Planeta—Espejo de la Argentina, 1995.

## *FICTION*

Puig, Manuel. *The Kiss of the Spider Woman*. Translated by Thomas Colchie, New York: Vintage, 1991.

Thornton, Lawrence. *Imagining Argentina*. New York: Doubleday, 1987.

—*Tales from the Blue Archives*. New York: Bantam, 1998.

## *VIDEO RECORDING*

Puenzo, Luis. *The Official Story*, New York: Fox Lorber Home Video, 1955.

# INDEX

Introductory note: Certain names, places and organizations appear so frequently throughout the book, that they are not indexed except for special events. These include Hebe de Bonafini herself, her husband and children, the Mothers of the Plaza de Mayo, and the Plaza itself.

## A

Albright, Madeleine 190, 191
Alfonsín, Raúl 154-169
Amnesty International 46, 94, 107, 192, 193, 208, 209
Amnesty Laws, see Law of Due Obedience, Final Point Law 162, 163

Anarchism 168
ANCLA, Latin American Clandestine News Agency 208
Anderson, Jon Lee 11
Aramburo, Pedro 35
Arditti, Rita 213
*Argentina Reader* 205, 207
Association of the Mothers of the Plaza de Mayo 117, 118
Association of Victims of Terrorism, AVT 191, 192
Astiz, Alfredo ("Gustavo") 93, 99, 100, 167, 210, 211
Azucena, [Villaflor de De Vicente] 72, 73, 78-80, 90, 91, 99-102, 141, 201

## B

Batista, Fulgenio 42
Bouvard, Marguerite Guzman 10, 164, 166-168
*Buenos Aires Herald,* newspaper 207
Bugnone, Maria Elena, wife of Jorge de Bonafini 47, 48, 63, 108

## C

*Cadena Informativa*, underground newspaper 208
Carter, Jimmy 177, 178
Castro, Fidel 42, 167, 189, 190
Catholic Church 14, 45, 152, 159, 180, 200

Center for Legal and Social Studies 209

Che, see Guevara

CONADEP, Argentine National Commission on the Disappeared 156, 157, 179, 193, 214

Cox, Robert 207

Cuba 167, 187, 189, 198, 201

de Bonafini, Alejandra, Hebe's daughter -birth, 37 d

de Bonafini, Humberto, ("Toto"), Hebe's husband—-courtship and marriage 29-31; death 143-148

de Bonafini, Jorge., Hebe's son, birth 31; marriage 63;disappearance 49,50 imprisonment 86,87 ; 120,121

de Bonafini, Raúl, Hebe's son, birth 34 ; disappearance 95-97; imprisonment 122-129

de Vincente, Azucena Villaflor, see Azucena

**D**

De la Rúa, Fernando 183-198

Delgado, Ariel 207

Diago, Alejandro 11, 135, 178

Doctrine of National Security, [United States] 68, 69, 187, 188

Domon, Alice 78,100,211

Duquet, Leonie 211

**E**

Elián, see González

Epelbaum, Renée 132

ESMA, Naval Mechanics School 45, 119, 180, 181

ETA, Basque terrorist group 191-193

Exhumations 163, 164, 213, 214

**F**

Falklands Islands, Malvinas Islands 142, 152, 174, 181

Feitlowitz, Marguerite 46, 213

Final Point Law 163

Fonda, Jane 175

Ford Foundation 214

Fox, Vicente 195, 196

Front for Human Rights 166, 167

**G**

Gandhi, Mohandas 11, 151

Garzón, Baltasar 191

Globalization 193-195

González, Elián 190

Granado, Alberto 198

Grandmothers of the Plaza de Mayo 122, 192, 212, 213

Grasselli, Father Emilio 72

Guevara, Ernesto "Che" 41, 42, 161, 167, 168, 187, 198, 200, 205

"Gustavo", see Astiz

**H**

Habeas Corpus 45, 54, 56-58, 64, 65, 68, 97, 152, 209,

Human Rights 15, 16, 154, 155, 171, 189, 199, 211, 212

Human Rights Day 94, 100-102

Human Rights Organizations 110, 175, 183, 190, 195, 209

Human rights violations 16, 46, 80, 112, 113

**I**

Imperialism 177, 178, 187, 188, 190, 205

International Monetary Fund 15, 65

International Conference on Cancer 110

**J**

Jorge, see de Bonafini, Jorge

Junta 46, 132, 193

**K**

Kaufman, Michael T. 215

Kennedy, Edward M. 107, 112, 115, 138

**L**

*La Nación*, newspaper 94, 95, 192

*La Opinión*, newspaper 207

La Tablada, revolt 168, 169

Laghi, Pio, Papal Nuncio 67, 136

*Las Locas,* Mothers' newspaper *13, 193*

Law of Due Obedience 162

League for Human Rights 72

Malvinas Islands, see Falklands Islands

**M**

Marcos, Commandante 195, 196, 202

Menem, Carlos Saul 169-183, 200

Mignone, Angelica 117

Mignone, Emilio 60, 61, 72, 209, 212

Mignone, Monica 209

Military and the Mothers of the Plaza de Mayo 135, 141, 142, 155, 156, 160, 164, 165, 180, 181

Military, trials of 157-159,179; pardons for, 168, 171; repression by, 13-16, 149, 150

Moreno, Mariano 25, 204

Mothers of the Plaza de Mayo—Founding Line 165, 166, 192

**N**

Neruda, Pablo 41

*New York Times* 196,197

Nobel Peace Prize 131, 132

Nouzeilles, Gabriela 10
*Nunca Más*, report of CONADEP 150, 156, 157, 179, 207

**O**

OAS Commission on Human Rights 116, 118, 211, 212
OAS, Organization of American States 94, 118, 119, 211, 212
*Official Story*, film 213
Operación Masacre 35, 205

**P**

*Para Tí*, women's weekly 107
People's Revolutionary University 186, 187, 198, 201
Perez, Esquivel Adolfo 131, 132
Permanent Assembly for Human Rights 72
Perón, Eva 210
Perón, Isabel 15
Perón, Juan Domingo 35
Pertini, Sandro 114
Pironi, Eduardo, Cardinal 114, 115
Plaza, Monsignor Antonio José 82,83
Ponce, Mary 78, 100
Pope Paul VI 110, 113, 114, 121, 174
Primatesta, Cardinal Francisco 67, 91, 106
Process for National Reorganization 44

**R**

Raúl, see de Bonafini, Raúl
Relatives of the Detained and Disappeared 99, 100
Rosenberg, Tina 211, 214
Russo, Leopoldo 57, 58, 64

**S**

Sábato, Ernesto 150, 157, 193, 211
Sanchez, Matilde 10, 13
Sarmiento, Domingo Faustino 25, 42, 204
Scilingo, Adolfo Francisco 179, 180
Seeger, Pete 175
Shirer, William L. 11
Snow, Clyde C. 214
Soros, George 193-5, 214, 215
Strassera, Julius Caesar 158

**T**

Thornton, Lawrence 213
Timerman, Jacobo 207, 211
Todman, Terence 79
Torture 45, 206, 207
Triple Alliance, (AAA), Argentine Anti-Communist Alliance 15, 184, 185

**U**

United Nations International Congress on Human Rights 177

United Nations, (UN) 177, 178,
189
United States 178, 187-190,
198, 201-202, 212, 215
University of Buenos Aires 181

## V

Vance, Cyrus 80
Verbitsky, Horatio 11, 179,
180, 212
Videla, Jorge 15, 68, 77, 79, 91,
92
Viñas, David 161

## W

Walsh, Rodolfo 5, 64, 65, 180,
205, 206
World Bank 187
World Cup, soccer championship 108-110, 142
World Trade Center, attack on
9/11/01 13, 197, 198, 201,
202

## Z

Zapatistas 176, 195, 196, 202